Aunt Harri Walks the Line

ALSO BY RAY WISEMAN:

I Cannot Dream Less

Aunt Harri Walks the Line

*and other adventures starring
the feisty oldster and her friends*

Ray Wiseman

Partners International
Brampton

WordWise Associates
Fergus

Published jointly by:

Partners International
8500 Torbram Road, Unit 48
Brampton, Ontario
Canada L6T 5C6

and

WordWise Associates
Fergus, Ontario

Printed in Canada

ISBN: 0-9698108-1-4

*The author pledges
$1.00 from the sale of this
book to the education of children
in third-world countries through the
Sponsor-A-Child program of Partners International.*

CONTENTS

ACKNOWLEDGEMENTS

Many people unknowingly contributed to this book. Without physically touching its pages during production, they prepared the way by encouraging my early writing. A thank you to the editors of various publications who saw fit to carry my columns, articles, and features. I owe a debt of gratitude to the staff of *The Guelph Daily Mercury* and *The Guelph Daily Mercury Seniors' Magazine* for ongoing support and encouragement. Two of them deserve special mention: Bob Zeller, whose counsel resulted in the introduction of Aunt Harri; and Valerie Hill whose enthusiastic response to each new Aunt Harri adventure fuelled my imagination and creativity.

Another special thank you to Grover Crosby of Partners International (PI) who entrusted me with the editing of *Partners* magazine and with major writing assignments. A definite thanks for the support and encouragement of the board of PI for allowing the publication of this book under their banner.

The greatest help of all came from Anna Wiseman. Not only does she appear in many episodes with Aunt Harri, Bert, and me, she proofread and edited her way through every line—first prior to original publication, and then as we selected columns for this book. How can one properly thank a partner of over 40 years? I must also mention the family members and friends who read my columns by E-mail before any editor sees them. I appreciate their commentary, criticism, wit, and encouragement—all of which help keep me on the straight and narrow.

INTRODUCTION

I had just seated myself in the optometrist's waiting room when the receptionist asked, "Tell me, is Aunt Harri a real person?" That question typifies many I have received from friends and total strangers since Aunt Harri's appearance as a regular in my monthly column for seniors. Although she has appeared in a number of publications aimed chiefly at seniors, she has carved out a place in the hearts of readers of all ages.

Aunt Harri's popularity prompted me to introduce Bert (only his mother would dare call him Egbert) as a monthly visitor in my weekly column. This opinionated, eccentric bachelor now has a following of his own—mostly among those who wish they had Bert's ability to thrust themselves into situations where only angels would dare to tread.

I have also included some columns dealing with family relationships. This whole book deals with relationships— relationships between generations, between men, and within families.

My column writing began when *The Guelph Mercury, Seniors Magazine* accepted my submissions, which eventually became the 'Aunt Harri' series. Within a year the newspaper asked me to produce a weekly opinion column, from which we have drawn most of the remaining chapters in this book.

Getting back to the question: "Is Aunt Harri a real person?" You decide. How could anyone that feisty, independent, and with such a complex history be anything but real?

Ray Wiseman, Fergus, Ontario

Aunt Harri Shares
her Golden Years

Aunt Harri Walks the Line

Turning to my wife, I said, "Look Anna, here comes our new neighbour. She must be two kilometres from home."

I pulled the car onto the shoulder while we watched Aunt Harri's progress toward us along the oiled road. She tapped her cane down briskly, using it more to keep her hand busy than to aid in walking. She marched along with the other hand swinging freely and her chin thrust forward. Only her slightly-stooped shoulders betrayed her age.

As we watched her approach, we remembered our first meeting only two weeks earlier. Arriving at our door the afternoon she moved in across the street, she had asked, "Can I borrow a hammer? I need to fix my bed."

As Anna went for the hammer, I offered, "I would be happy to give you a hand."

"No," she said. "I can do it myself—thank you."

She had added the thank you almost as an afterthought, while looking me up and down. She struck me as slightly arrogant, maybe just independent. Then as though sensing we might think her rude, she smiled and said, "I'm sorry. My name is Harriet, but you can call me Aunt Harri. All the other young folks call me Aunt Harri."

The words "young folk" had caught me off guard. I just hit 60, and I won't tell you Anna's age. I can only describe Aunt Harri as of indeterminate age. Now as she approached us on the road, I wondered if I dare offer her a ride.

I rolled down the window and said, "Aunt Harri. It's still ten kilometres to town."

"I am not . . .," she began, but recognizing my teasing tone, she continued, "Just out for a brisk walk. Do it every day. Believe in keeping in shape. Best way is walking."

Noting the shortness of Aunt Harri's breath, I dared offer, "We can give you a ride back, if you like."

"No, I'm fine. I'll pause for just a moment," she answered, leaning against the car. For a long moment she seemed to stare off into the distance. We kept silent.

"Some of those old people over there," she said pointing her stick toward our community of middle-aged and retired people, "don't have the brains to keep in shape. They sit on their butts all summer, then do the same all winter in Florida or Arizona."

I wanted to challenge her on that one. How could she judge people in a community in only two weeks? Before I could answer, she said, "You might wonder how I know. I have eyes. Last week, the man next door actually got out of his deck chair, took off his shirt and mowed his tiny lawn. Never saw anything so disgusting in all my life. Him 50 pounds overweight with his big beer belly swinging out over his belt. Disgusting! If I wanted a husband, I certainly wouldn't look for one here. If they would keep in shape, think of the millions the government would save in medical costs."

After a moment's silence again, she went on, "I learned to walk in the army. They made us stay in shape—marched us for miles, then expected a full day's work."

I think the look of disbelief on Anna's face brought further explanation, for Aunt Harri said, "I was a WAAC. Cooked for the boys when they went up the line to the trenches. Had to be in shape. Used my fists once or twice back then, and you never know today when you might get mugged, so I keep fit."

Without another word, she nodded and moved briskly on her way. Her voice drifted back on the wind; I could hear a mezzo soprano singing a marching song to the beat of a cane: "I had a good home and I left . . . left . . . left."

Anna looked at me in wonder and said, "From what she said, from the words and description, that woman was talking about the First World War! She must be in her nineties!"

Watching the retreating, elderly, but energetic figure, I said, "Yes, either that or the Anglo-Boer War."

Driving Aunt Harri

I answered the front door to see Aunt Harri leaning heavily on her cane and supporting a large paper-wrapped parcel in her free arm. Inviting her in, I motioned her to the sofa just inside the front door. I knew better than to offer my new neighbour help, so I ignored the parcel. I did notice a city name and address inked clearly on the wrapper.

"I am sending it to my great-grandson for his first birthday," Aunt Harri said as she sat down.

"Oh," I said, but wondered why she had brought it to my place. I didn't speculate long; she just went ahead in her brusque style.

"You go into town often. Could you take this to the post office and mail it? I'll give you money for stamps."

"I can do better than that," I answered. We plan a trip to the city this afternoon. Come with us and deliver it personally."

Even though I fully expected her to refuse my offer, that afternoon Aunt Harri and her parcel squeezed into the back seat of our little car. As we drove along the county road toward town, a large car suddenly turned from a side road into our lane without as much as a glance our way from the grey-haired driver. I braked sharply, throwing Aunt Harri's parcel to the floor. Thanks to the seat belt she didn't follow after it. With no damage done we followed the offender at ridiculously slow speeds, only getting ahead after entering the main highway near town.

Aunt Harri glared at the driver and, in a voice almost loud enough for him to hear, said, "Stupid old coot. If you can't do better than that turn in your driver's licence."

Mindful of my own grey hair, I said, "Surely we can be a little patient with older drivers."

Aunt Harri snapped back, "Not if they threaten my life."

"Did you ever drive?" I asked her.

She settled back in the seat, stared off into the distance and began to talk: "Tried to drive the Willys-Overland, back on the farm in Alberta. When I first tried, I froze at the wheel and raced in circles around the well. Good thing I didn't straighten out or I might have shot down the coulee bank and killed myself. Fred jumped on the running board and stopped the thing. I didn't try again for years."

I let her sit quietly for a moment, but smelling a good story, I prompted her: "When did you learn to drive?"

"Just before the war," she answered. "Fred died. He was 20 years older than me. I decided to move to Ontario to be near my sister. Bought a '29 Model A, learned to drive it, loaded up the three kids, and hit the road. My oldest boy, he was about 12, had the knack to keep the thing running. That was an adventure. We had little money so slept in the car most times. Sometimes people offered us a place to stay. Took us three weeks, even though we cut through the States; Canadian roads were vile then."

"Go on," I prompted.

"Made that trip four more times during the late forties and fifties. We had to get back to check on the farm and see relatives. Then my oldest son helped with the driving. In '48 bought a '39 Ford V8; took it out twice. Then we went twice in the 51 Austin. Got to know US Route 2 like an old friend."

"Do you still drive?" I asked.

"No," she said incredulously, I gave that up in '73,

twenty years ago. Took my daughter to visit a friend. On the
return trip, I drove through a stop sign and nearly hit a truck.
It shook us up. My daughter said that I had run through two
other stops on that trip."

She paused, then went on without prompting: "Two days
later the three kids and their mates arrived at my place, sat me
down, and told me to give up my driver's licence. I'll never
forget their shocked looks when I said, 'You're too late. I
turned it in yesterday.'"

Aunt Harri chuckled to herself, before saying, "It was
time to quit driving. But I make my own decisions. Don't
need that kind of help from family or anyone else."

Aunt Harri Turns Green

One day last spring, I went into the garden to rake up refuse,
putting it together in a tidy heap beside the tiny vegetable
garden. Our community had informed us that garden refuse
was our problem, saying in a newsletter, "Compost it."

"You will have to get one of those plastic composters," a
voice behind me said.

I turned to see my neighbour, the candid and spontaneous
Aunt Harri. Before I could respond, she pointed her cane at
my lilies and said, "Came in for a closer look. Very
colourful."

"Thank you Harriet," I answered.

"Also thought you might like to read this book on the
environment," she said handing me a paperback. Without
saying another word, she turned, climbed the two steps to my
deck, and dropped into a chair. She then positioned herself so
she could see the lilies and watch the finches at the bird
feeder.

Feeling as though a higher authority had bidden me, I put down the rake, mounted the steps, and sat in the other chair. I waited for her to speak.

After a few moments, she said, "Your Virginia creeper looks good. There is a lot of rubbish in there."

Puzzled, I asked, "In the Virginia creeper?"

"No! In that book I gave you on the environment."

"Oh!" I responded. "Don't you believe in protecting God's creation?"

She nodded her head, "Believe in it very much. I just don't like the way they blame previous generations for the mess the world is in. We are all guilty, but some of us less than the present generation."

"Explain yourself," I challenged.

"Humph," she snorted, "Fred and I practised the three Rs, reduce, reuse, and recycle, long before the modern generation thought they invented them. Actually, we never concerned ourselves with the first one, reduce, because we never had the money to buy in excess to begin with. Never had the materialistic bent of modern young people either. We certainly did reuse and recycle."

"Give me some examples," I prompted.

"Take clothing," she began. "When the oldest boy finished wearing something, I passed it on to the next. Then the neighbours got it. When no one could wear it, it became cleaning rags. Take garden refuse; we dug that back into the ground, burning the noxious weeds. All of the kitchen refuse, we called that slop, went to the pigs. They recycled it into ham and bacon."

"What about packaging materials?" I asked.

"Didn't have much of that," she answered. "Things like sugar and flour came in large white bags. We saved the bags, bleached them and turned them into pillowcases, and sometimes made items of clothing. Peanut butter and honey came in pails. Small pails are always handy around a farm. I

used the glass jars for preserves, sealing the tops with wax.
Every weekend we got the Star Weekly. Big paper with a
number of sections. After we read it, Fred rolled it tightly into
small doughnut shapes and burned it in the Quebec heater
during the cold weather."

"What about pollution from cars and machinery?" I asked.

"Fred used mostly horses. He spread the 'pollution' on
the fields as fertilizer. When a machine wore out, Fred or a
neighbour would cut it up to make something else. Almost
everyone had a wagon made from the running gear of an old
car. One Christmas we got a toboggan for the kids. A friend
made it from a long metal advertising sign; just rolled it up at
one end and attached a rope. On the underside it had a
beautiful enamelled finish with the word 'Firestone.' Heavy to
pull up a hill, but nothing could beat it going down."

"So what do you say to people today?" I inquired as Aunt
Harri got up to leave.

"Don't waste your time blaming your parents and grand-
parents. Just get on with the job of cleaning up the mess
caused by materialism and greed."

She started down the steps, then turned to say one thing
more: "All of us older ones will help. After all it is partly our
fault; we raised a selfish and indifferent generation."

Romancing Aunt Harri

I looked up to see Aunt Harri coming across the street at ten
o'clock on a Tuesday. She had swung into her army walk, her
cane snapping down smartly on the gravel. Her head thrust
forward gave her a look of determination. Either something
had gone wrong with the nonagenarian, or she had some
exciting news to share.

"Anna," I cried out, "put some more boiling water on the tea bag. Here comes Aunt Harri."

I slid the door open before Harriet could knock, startling her. "Come in," I said, "We just put the kettle on." Right then, I realized I had begun to enjoy visits from my crusty neighbour.

Aunt Harri sat down at the kitchen table, folded her hands under her chin and rested her elbows on the table. She said nothing, but had a far-away look on her face. I itched to ask what was up, but thought it better to wait.

"I can't believe it," she began, wagging her head. "After all these years! It's like a ghost from the past."

"Exactly what are you talking about?" I ventured.

"Hubert," she answered, as though that explained everything. I decided to revert to the waiting game.

After a moment she went on: "I met Hubert in my teens, before I joined the WAACs and left England for France to cook in the Great War. He came courting me on his motorcycle. And don't give me that funny look, we had motorbikes back then! Mind you it was different from a modern machine. Had to run beside it and jump on to get it started. Anyway, one day he took me for a ride down a country road. Somehow he missed a curve and spilled me into a patch of stinging nettles. Swore off motorcycles for life after that."

"Did you swear off Hubert?" I asked.

"Not then. After the war, he asked me to marry him. I turned him down because he was a bit wild, drank you know. Anyway, I wanted to emigrate to Canada. It would never have worked because our interests were so different. At least I tell myself that. I moved to Canada and Hubert just vanished into history."

At this point Anna joined the conversation: "What happened to bring all this to mind? Did you dream about Hubert last night?"

Aunt Harri gave us a stunned look. "Didn't I tell you? Yesterday a car pulled into my driveway and an elderly man I didn't know from Adam came to my door, leaving a young woman waiting in the car. I answered the knock, assuming he had the wrong place. He didn't speak, just stood there for a moment. I asked him a little curtly what he wanted. Then he said in a proper British voice, 'Harriet, don't you recognize me? I'm Hubert.'"

Anna and I quietly digested that. Aunt Harri soon continued her story: "I invited him to stay for tea and cake. He asked the young woman, his granddaughter, to bring the car back later. Then he sat down as though he owned the place and we picked up on the conversation we had left off 70 years ago. He said, 'I quit drinking. I wrote and told you, but you never answered so I married Florence.' Of course I never got his letter, not that it would have made any difference. After dinner his granddaughter returned and beeped the car horn. As he stood up to leave, he said, 'I lost Flo 20 years ago. I'm lonely. Harriet, will you marry me?' I just blurted out, 'Hubert, you old fool, get out of here!'"

Aunt Harri looked puzzled and distraught for a few moments, then grabbed her cane and headed for the door. Halfway through she suddenly turned back and said, "Oh, I forgot to ask you the question that brought me here. Could you take me into the hairdresser this afternoon? Hubert asked me out for dinner tonight."

The Voice of an Angel

A young man stood at my door with a parcel in his arms and a slightly puzzled look on his face. He said, "I have a parcel for Mrs. Harriet Brown, across the street, but I can't get an answer although I can hear a radio or something."

"I'll handle it," I answered, taking the parcel. I immediately started across the street, a sense of concern gripping me. I had often worried about Aunt Harri living alone in her nineties. I had hoped the arrival of her childhood sweetheart would correct that concern, but she had said no more about him.

I raised my hand to knock, but froze on the spot. I could hear music, music with a haunting, plaintiff sound. I leaned close to the glass, looked in, and saw Aunt Harri. She stood at the kitchen cupboard, hands resting on the counter, her face toward the window. I sensed she was looking, not out of the window, but at something distant, something in another world. Her voice, a rich mezzo soprano, sang:

"Why should I feel discouraged,
Why should the shadows come,
Why should my heart be lonely,
And long for Heaven and home . . ."

On the word discouraged, her voice dropped, low, rich, beautiful, yet with great emotion, almost as though she were pleading for something. I thought, "Aunt Harri, you can sing; you have been keeping something from us."

At that moment she stopped singing and turned away from the window, revealing a look of deep sorrow. I stepped back quickly and rapped on the glass door.

"Come in, come in," she said brightly, but gave me a look that suggested she knew I had listened.

I gave her the parcel and explained its origin. She thanked me and motioned to a chair.

"I guess I didn't hear the delivery man. I was singing; it's my way of communing with God. Especially when my spirits need lifting," she volunteered.

"Is something wrong?" I asked.

"Yes it is; I am afraid I have been a great fool."

"Can I help?"

"Maybe if you just listen it would help," she said. "I should never have bought this place. I really can't look after it. I thought I had made my last move coming here, last that is before the really big move when I go home."

She said the word home with a sense of awe or longing. I sat quietly and let her continue.

"My eyes are going. Lost one when a blood vessel broke in it a few years ago, sort of like a stroke. Now the doctor says I have macular degeneration in the other. I may lose most of my sight in a year or two. And I'm just tired. I get fed up with being alone, with making meals for one, with being stuck out here so far away from my family and friends. I guess this old war horse has been just too stubborn and independent."

I saw a single tear run down her cheek. Suddenly the old Aunt Harri returned. As though embarrassed that she had dropped her guard in front of a near-stranger, she stood to her feet and said almost curtly, "Thank you for bringing the parcel."

I rose to leave, but before I could get through the door she spoke again, using a softer tone: "Thank you for staying a moment to hear me out. I shouldn't complain." She paused for a moment, then said emphatically, "I'm not really alone."

As I turned to slide the door to, I noticed she had returned to her strange pose by the counter and window. Before I could pull the door the last few inches, she had begun to sing again. I stepped backwards to move out of her sight and listened. This time her voice had more power and brightness; It had a quality that rang with hope and victory:

"I sing because I'm happy,
 I sing because I'm free,
 For His eye is on the sparrow,
 And I know He watches me."

Aunt Harri Remembers

One November, James—our oldest grandchild—asked Aunt Harri, "What does that red flower mean?"

Aunt Harri looked down at the poppy in the lapel of her jacket and began caressing it gently with one finger. She remained silent for so long we thought we had made a big mistake inviting her to meet our grandson. We wondered if a crusty 96-year-old could bridge the multiple generation gap.

His voice quiet and concerned, James tried again, "Aunt Harri?"

Aunt Harri answered quietly, "It means I remember. Remember the war and those who died. Went with the women's army to France during the First World War, the Great War we called it."

"You were a lady soldier? Did you shoot people?" James shot back incredulously.

Aunt Harri laughed as she answered, "Oh no. We went to war as cooks, nurses, and clerks. They didn't give us guns; we fought the war with cooking pots, bed pans, and notebooks."

"Was it fun?" James asked.

"Fun? War is never fun. It's pain and death and horror. It's fear and sickness . . .," Aunt Harri paused for a long moment, stared at James and then went on. "Yes and it is fun when you're young and away from home for the first time." She rapped her cane on the footstool and said, "Sit here James and I'll tell you how the Jerries attacked the city near our camp almost every day with their airplanes."

James cut in, "What are Jerries?"

"Germans, the enemy then. We called their airplanes 'air-bombers.' When the sirens sounded we ran for cover in underground rooms called air-raid shelters. Each air-bomber carried two bombs on a teeter-totter thing. The airman pushed one bomb off and the other fell a few seconds later. One evening we girls had just made it into the shelter when a bomb fell near the camp. Most of us froze in terror, knowing the next might be closer—could kill us all. But nothing scared Emily. She sat on a ledge half-way up the wall, laughing, and taunting, 'Jerries can't hit nothing; Jerries can't hit nobody.'

"Just then the second bomb exploded outside, blasting us all against the far wall. I saw Emily flying end-over-teakettle into the middle of the room, landing on the dirt floor. She got up, shook herself and said, 'I don't mind Jerry dropping his bombs. But I wish he wouldn't throw dirt in my face.' The rest of us forgot our fear and roared with laughter."

James asked, "Why did they attack a camp full of women?"

"Didn't know we were women, I guess. Our boys, the British army, had placed guns on nearby hills to shoot at the air-bombers. One day as the airplanes attacked the city, the soldiers at one gun loaded and fired as fast as they could into the air above our camp. The shells exploded above us like fireworks as we ran for the shelter. We later heard that a senior officer rushed up to the gun crew and yelled, 'Don't fire that way; the bombers are over the city. There are no planes where you're firing.' The captain in charge of the gun roared back, 'No there aren't, and there aren't going to be; that's where the girls are!"

"Wow," I wish I could have been there firing the gun," James said with enthusiasm.

In response Aunt Harri struck her cane on the floor, then fell strangely silent. Her face hardened, and her eyes stared at an empty space on the far wall. James, thinking he had offended her stole away. After a minute that seemed like ten, she spoke: "Why do we do that? Why do we glorify war to each new generation? Why do we laugh at things that are no laughing matter?" She became quiet again.

After a few moments, I ventured "We laugh at our own fear."

"Possibly," Aunt Harri answered. "Either that, or we laugh to cover the shame. The shame that all sides should feel, that civilized people could act in such barbaric ways."

Without another word, Aunt Harri left. I watched her cross the street, her figure more bent than usual, carrying the burdens of more than ninety years—hers and the world's.

A Home for Aunt Harri

Early one Monday morning in December as I sat at breakfast, I looked out to see Aunt Harri feeling her way carefully down her front steps. The moment both feet reached the level ground, she moved quickly away at her typical military pace. Her right hand held her ever-present cane. Her left grasped a number of envelopes.

"Our neighbour is out early to post some mail," I said to no one in particular.

During the next couple of weeks we saw Aunt Harri make her way daily on the dot of twelve to the community postboxes—a time that guaranteed the mailman had made his visit. It didn't surprise us to see her sending and receiving letters; what captured our imagination was the look of grim determination on her face. We now knew our neighbour well enough to know when she did something, she did it with a vengeance.

About three weeks after observing Harriet's regular jaunts, I happened to meet her at the mailboxes. As I opened my box, she busily stuffed junk mail into the ever-hungry garbage can put there for that purpose. "Hello Aunt Harri," I said.

She muttered a response and, empty-handed and grim-faced, started for home. I watched her retreating figure for a moment and thought, "Something has got under the old girl's skin."

Back at home I began to look through my mail: three bills, one rejection slip, a card for Anna, and a letter addressed to Mrs. Harriet Brown. The mailman had erred, putting Aunt Harri's letter in my box. The envelope, important looking, sported an attractive logo and return address: Village Mews Retirement Home. Remembering Aunt Harri's loneliness, failing eyesight, and grim demeanour in recent days, I immediately put on my coat and hat and started across the street. I had a feeling this letter might have great importance to her.

She came to the door with her mouth set in a straight line, her brow wrinkled. For once she looked her years.

"The mailman left this in my box by mistake," I ventured.

"Thank you," she said regaining some of her old brightness. "Been expecting it for days."

"Is something wrong? Can I help?" I asked.

"Come in for a moment. You're so kind," she answered with only a hint of hesitation. Actually that bothered me a little, for I realized my interest might have more to do with curiosity than kindness.

She motioned to a chair and immediately began to speak: "Made the decision to move to an old-folks home. Been writing and asking questions for weeks. Tough decision, but I now know I can't stay on alone. Eyes nearly gone, you know. Should move somewhere and learn my way about when I can still see. Kids can't take me—no room. Wouldn't want to impose anyway. Asked all three. Got the same answer, 'We'd love to have you Mother, but we have no room.' Sort of like the Christmas story, isn't it?"

"The Christmas story?" I answered, puzzled.

"Yes, no room at the inn," she said. "Oh, I haven't read my mail." With that she produced a knitting needle from a bag at her side and slit the envelope open. She seemed to forget my presence while she read the letter, holding it close to her best eye.

"They want me to come. They have a room for me," Aunt Harri finally said. "It's from the Village Mews Retirement Home. What does the word 'mews' mean?"

I answered, "Originally the word referred to a row of stables in an English town. Today, most mews in England have become garages or apartments. In Canada people use the word just to sound British."

Aunt Harri's mouth arced into the first smile I had seen on her face in weeks. "A stable," she said. "Then I will be in good company won't I—there is room in the stable."

Thanks, but No Thanks

During the winter, Aunt Harri's deep mezzo tones resonated over the phone: "Would you be free to take me to visit a seniors' home today? Got a letter from another one yesterday. Said they wanted to see me and me to see their place. It's not far away—not 20 minutes drive."

"When would you like to go?" I asked. We settled on early afternoon. At 1:30 we pulled up in front of a rather bleak, wind-swept building bearing a sign that said, "Sunset Country Manor—A Home for Seniors."

Leaning into the January wind, we headed through the snow toward the front door, Anna and I flanking Aunt Harri. We knew better than offer help; she could take an arm if she felt the need. Too late I noticed the ice beneath the snow; both feet shot forward and I crashed backward to the ground. Out of the corner of my eye, I saw another body fall. For a moment I lay motionless staring skyward, but a strange gurgling sound brought me to my senses. I sat up to see Aunt Harri trying to stifle laughter as she helped Anna to her feet.

Neither of us had suffered injury, except to our pride. Aunt Harri latched onto our arms as if to steady us and said, "Maybe all three of us are ready to check into this place."

Inside we met the middle-aged matron or superintendent, who gushed, "Hello, I'm Eleanor Green. You must be Harriet. You came to look us over."

"Mrs. Harriet Brown," Aunt Harri snapped. The matron's familiarity had wiped away the good humour sparked by our calamity of moments before.

The rebuke never registered on Mrs. Green. She continued gushing in a too-familiar way while leading us on a tour of the facility. Throwing open a door to a room she spoke directly to me, "Your Aunt would have a room just like this one. Notice the adjoining washroom. And, of course, she could bring her own furniture."

"She's not really our Aunt. She is . . .," I tried to cut in, but Green continued gushing.

Looking at Anna, she said: "We provide a hospital-style bed, but Harriet could bring her furniture. We find the old folks like to have their own things around them. It makes the move much easier for them."

With that she led us to the dining room with Aunt Harri tagging along behind. The matron stopped at one of the tables already set for the evening meal. She turned to me and said, "Our guests remain at the same tables during their stay with us. That helps them to become close friends with a few of the others. It helps them become part of a new family."

As we walked toward the kitchen, the matron turned to me and said, "You will have to tell us if your Aunt needs any special diet. We try to meet all special needs of our guests."

I turned to speak to Aunt Harri, but saw her parked on a chair in the dining room glaring after us. After a quick tour of the kitchen, we picked up Aunt Harri and headed back to the foyer, stopping in front of a nursing station. I could feel my muscles and nerves still quivering from my fall, so I leaned against the counter. Aunt Harri had stopped just behind me, leaning on her cane beside a large brass urn holding three or four blades of pampas grass.

The matron spoke to Anna, "If you could fill us in on Harriet's health requirements, we could assume the responsibility to dispense her medications."

Suddenly, a loud metallic crash, like someone striking a huge gong, filled the room. My legs buckled so I had to support myself on the counter. When I recovered, I turned to look at Aunt Harri. The brass urn still rocked slightly. Aunt Harri lowered her cane from a baseball-batter's grip, leaned on it and glared at a speechless Eleanor Green. A dozen employees of the home gathered around us.

Aunt Harri spoke in a strong, controlled voice: "Mrs. Green, I am a thinking, breathing, feeling person just like you. I am quite capable of making my own decisions and picking my own friends. I may be elderly, but my brain works as well as it did 50 years ago. I can answer personally for my diet and my medical needs. I am not interested in becoming part of your gulag. Good day!"

With that she turned and marched out into the snow. Thinking the situation demanded a special exit, I bowed, tipped my hat to the matron, and hurried after Aunt Harri. She might need help when she reached the icy patch.

Aunt Harri Learns a Lesson

Our relationship with Aunt Harri became much closer the day
she nearly burned her house down. Anna and I, without hats
or coats, hurried across the street on a wild winter day in
answer to her call.

A visibly shaken Harriet Brown answered the door. "Set
fire to my kitchen stove. Set a box of rice on the back burner
when the phone rang. Came back, forgot the box, filled the
kettle and put it on the front burner. Then I foolishly lit the
wrong gas burner. Soon I had flames. Had presence of mind
to turn off the burner and pour the kettle on the fire. Have I
damaged my stove?"

"No, we can help you clean that up," I answered. "But I'd
worry more about you than the stove. You could have killed
yourself. With your bad eyes you shouldn't use the stove."

"I shouldn't be here. Should move to the seniors'
residence. But I can't seem to make up my mind. I put off
making a decision till spring," Aunt Harri explained, her
hands still shaking from her experience.

Anna coaxed her to her favourite chair, then asked,
"Couldn't you get meals sent in? From Meals on Wheels or
some other group?"

Aunt Harri answered, "I tried that. They don't deliver out
here in the country. Too far from town. When I bought here I
never thought that one day I might need services that aren't
available."

"Then you had better eat your evening meal with us.
When the weather is bad, we can bring it across," Anna said,
giving me a look that indicated who would do the transporting
in bad weather.

"Oh, I couldn't do that . . .," Harri started, hesitated momentarily, then continued, "I'd have to pay you."

We soon made the arrangements and that very evening a more-relaxed and personable Aunt Harri joined us. The conversation around the dinner table heralded many more that were to follow.

Aunt Harri comfortably parked her elbows on the table and sipped from her tea cup held in both hands. She began to speak: "Don't know why I can't make up my mind about moving to a seniors' home. Always been able to make decisions. Mind you, made most decisions because I was stubborn. Wouldn't listen. Even in the army, I told them where to get off if I didn't agree. Maybe that's my problem —just too stubborn."

I started to comment, but Aunt Harri didn't hear me. She just continued with her story: "Went to France from England with the Women's Army Auxiliary Corps, the WAACs. Hadn't been there but a few months when they lined us up and made a big announcement. Told us we had a new name, Queen Mary's Army Auxiliary Corps. They handed us new badges for our hats with the letters, QMAAC. Was I mad! She wouldn't give us her name when we first went to France. We had to bear all the gossip and criticism about our real purpose; some dared to suggest the army sent us just as a convenience for the men. Now that we had proved ourselves, she wanted us to wear her badge."

Aunt Harri paused for a sip of tea, then continued, "I threw the blame thing in the mud in France. I imagine it's still there over 75 years later. I wore my WAAC badge for the rest of the war. No one said a thing."

As she took another drink, I noticed a twinkle in her eye. Aunt Harri actually glowed as she continued: "Then one day an officer came to tell us he was assigning us to new duties. We had signed on as cooks. He told us we had to work in the officers' mess, serving officers. I said, 'No bloody way'—pardon the language. I had signed up as a cook, not as a waitress to a bunch of . . . well never mind. I just wouldn't do it. Two other girls and I went on strike, refused to follow orders. The officers didn't know what to do to us. Had we been men, I suppose they would have flogged us or shot us. Being a woman used to have real advantages."

Aunt Harri paused long enough to refill her cup, then continued, "The others finally gave in. I held out for another three weeks before they assigned me back to the kitchens. They said, 'This will go into your record.'"

Aunt Harri paused again before saying, "Maybe it's time I became a little less stubborn."

I thought, "Maybe we have much to learn from Aunt Harri."

Aunt Harri Speaks Wisdom

"Always make out a will," Aunt Harri said just before putting a forkful of dessert into her mouth. After Aunt Harri started eating her evening meals with Anna and me, life got interesting. She would suddenly introduce a new topic, then follow through with keen insight.

She let us wait for her pearls of wisdom until she had finished her mouthful: "Always make out a will. Doesn't matter how old or young you are. Also have a proper, legal power of attorney in case your partner goes off mentally. If you don't, the public administrator grabs everything. I know. It happened to me."

Stunned, I stared at Aunt Harri, unable to imagine her mentally incompetent at any time in her life.

"No," she said, almost as if she had read my mind, "I wasn't the one with problems. My husband became mentally

ill. He had everything in his name and he had no will or
power of attorney to protect us from the public administrator.
There I sat on the farm on the prairie with three kids and
almost no earnings. Public administrator grabbed everything.
Took the income from the farm. Left us with nothing. I
would like to believe that couldn't happen today, but if you
let a government bureaucrat in the door, you'll never get him
out. Had some terrible experiences before my husband died."

"How did you survive?" I asked.

"Only through God sending helpful people my way. He
even sent an angel dressed in a Mountie's uniform." With
that, a faraway look came into her eyes, and she chuckled.

"You seem to be able to laugh in the worst of
circumstances," I said.

"You must laugh, or you'd never make it through the
rough parts of life," she responded.

"Tell us about the mountie," I asked.

Aunt Harri paused for a moment, as though reviewing a
difficult time of her life. She began to speak slowly and
deliberately: "My husband became ill. We had nothing. My
doctor told me to pack up the kids and get out or I'd join my
husband in the asylum. Decided to sell my few belongings
and move to Ontario to live near my sister. Figured I could
find work. I put a notice up in the town store with a sale date
on it and waited for offers.

"Before the day arrived, a mountie came to my door. The
RCMP act as provincial police in Alberta. The mountie said,
'The Alberta public administrator sent me to tell you that you
can't sell and move away. You can't sell anything that
belongs to your husband.' That made me mad.

"I let him know I didn't plan to sell anything that
belonged to my husband. I marched him into the living room
and showed him the couch I had bought with money I had
made plucking turkeys for the local butcher. I pointed to the
cream separator I had bought with money earned cutting

vegetables for the local hospital. I led him around the house
explaining the other things I planned to sell. Then I asked
him, 'Are these my things or my husband's?'

"He said, 'Yours ma'am.' Then he stood at attention by
the door and put on his boy-scout hat, and said, 'Ma'am, the
public administrator sent me to tell you that you can't sell up
and leave.' Then he took off his hat, placed it over his heart,
smiled, and said, 'I spoke officially as a policeman. Now I'll
speak as a man. Go ahead—sell your things and move. They
can't touch you.' Then he bowed and walked out the door."

"Did you leave?" I asked.

"Certainly did. And that young policeman's attitude
encouraged me to plug on, to stand up for what was mine."

As though she had said too much, Aunt Harri gathered
her things and headed home. I immediately picked up the
phone and began dialling.

"Who are you calling," Anna asked.

I answered, "My friend Jim. Maybe he can recommend a
lawyer so we can update our wills and sign appropriate power
of attorney documents."

"Which one of us do you expect to become mentally
incompetent?" she asked.

When Jim said "Hello," I couldn't speak—not while I had
my tongue sticking out at Anna.

Aunt Harri Tells a Story

After finishing her evening meal, Aunt Harri in typical
fashion, headed to the closet to get her coat and Scottish tam.
However, this time she stopped in front of the piano and
stared at it as though searching back through years of
memories. After a moment she pushed back the keyboard

cover and began tapping out a tune with one finger. "Used to play one of these things. Quit my lessons and sold the piano. Should have continued. What you learn as a young person stays into old age.

Aunt Harri picked out a few more notes and sang:
"Bless this house, oh Lord we pray,
Make it safe by night and day . . ."

As she sang, I imagined how she must have sounded in youth: a powerful mezzo voice filling a room or church, lamps and windows vibrating in resonance, and listeners on the edge of their chairs. As I listened and imagined, I realized she almost always sang hymns—and occasionally old army or comedy songs. When she sang she lifted the spirits or made you laugh. And she sang often, even on the days when she confided in us that her arms and legs ached with arthritis.

She quit singing and said, "Should have taken voice lessons too. If I had I could sing better now. As I said, what you learn in your youth, even what you become when you're young, remains with you for life."

Aunt Harri turned to leave, but stopped and leaned on her cane with her other hand on the door handle. Looking back at us, she said, "Let me tell you a story. About 15 years ago, I heard that an old friend, Hannah, had moved in with her daughter. Hannah had always been difficult, even in her younger years. For old times sake, I went to see her."

Aunt Harri paused for a moment and bit her lower lip as if questioning whether she should continue.

She did go on: "Hadn't seen her for years. Got to the house, and Hannah's daughter, a haggard-looking soul in her fifties, took me to Hannah's room. Hannah snapped at me, said I should have come sooner, then asked me to sit down. Before I could say a word, Hannah started screaming at her daughter, asking which pill was the heart pill, the green one or the white one. The daughter, Helen, graciously pointed out the correct pill.

"For the next twenty minutes, Hannah complained about her daughter and son-in-law who, she said, didn't look after her properly. Then she started to yell for Helen to bring some tea. Helen brought it in about five minutes. Hannah asked what took all the time. When I left after another half hour of complaining, I paused at the door to say goodbye to Helen. Helen told me that her mother made life a living hell for her and her husband. As I went out the door I could hear Hannah yelling, 'What are you two talking about?' When I got outside I nearly cried."

As we listened to Aunt Harri's story her eyes clouded over. She stood for a minute, then said, "I went back a few more times, but I couldn't continue. Hannah began saying hurtful things to me, and continued to treat her daughter like dirt. Soon she lost me as a friend. We were the same age. I was too old to take that kind of abuse. Six months later Hannah died of a stroke."

Aunt Harri turned and walked the three steps back to the piano. She picked out a few more notes with one finger, then turned back to us.

"That's it," she said. "What you learn when you are young continues throughout your life. What you become as a young person, you remain even when you're 70, 80, or 90. If you're sweet and kind, you'll stay sweet and kind. If you're self-centred and miserable, no one will want to be near you when you get old. I didn't even go to Hannah's funeral."

Aunt Harri clicked her cane down hard as she stepped back to the door. Part way out she paused, looked back at us and said, "I can be difficult at times. But I pray to God, if I ever get even a little bit like Hannah that God will take me."

"I don't think you need to worry about that," Anna called after her. But Aunt Harri, singing a marching song, didn't hear. She clicked down the front steps and started across the gravel driveway, moving much too quickly for someone in her nineties.

Outwitted by Aunt Harri

After months of contemplating, Aunt Harri decided to move to a seniors' home. From our front window we watched the action on the lawn of her house. Her great-niece, Margo, arranged things on two tables: assorted dishes and cooking utensils, a fairly new crock pot, an old toaster, some bottles of preserves, brick-a-brack, garden tools, lamps, books, and pictures. Aunt Harri stood at the end of one table, giving commands, gesticulating with her cane, watching the collected memories of decades ready for exposure to the greedy eyes of strangers.

A sign said "YARD SALE - 9 A.M." Another small sign said "MORE INSIDE," and other tiny signs indicated the price of each item. Two cars occupied by impatient couples waited on the street. One car contained an overweight, older couple; the other held a younger seedy-looking pair. Both cars had arrived at eight o'clock before Margo had started loading the tables. We had watched with glee as Aunt Harri had driven them off with her imposing presence and threatening cane.

Now satisfied that the action could start, she waved at the waiting cars, prompting the occupants to leap to the street and close in like vultures with the sniff of decaying flesh in their nostrils. We grabbed our jackets and followed along, hoping we looked more like doves than vultures. Three other neighbours also joined the parade.

As I began to sort through old books, I noticed the seedy couple questioning Aunt Harri. She pointed toward the back door and said, "Just inside, left into the bedroom."

I watched Margo follow them discreetly. Looking toward

the other table, I saw the overweight couple piling colourful pieces of glassware and china into a bushel basket. My next-door neighbour placed a collection of garden tools into a pile for his wife to watch while he went to examine the lawnmower. Anna and I decided to go inside to see what had attracted the seedy couple.

As we reached the door they came out, followed by Margo. I glanced about the room to see a few items of furniture bearing price tags — nothing of interest there. I almost left without seeing the brown-paper wrappings on the bed. Inside I found four old picture frames, dust covered from years of storage. I slipped them part way from the wrapping. The first frame held nothing; the second contained a poorly-painted landscape; the third was an amateur's portrait of a much-younger Aunt Harri.

The fourth picture caused me to suck in my breath. My hand began to shake as I hissed out the words, "Anna, this is a Cornelius Krieghoff!"

I stared in wonder at a Quebec farm scene, a box-like sleigh, a happy couple, and an ice-covered river. My mind ran at a furious pace: buy this before someone else does; offer her whatever she wants; it could be worth thousands; but she won't know that.

As I slipped the dusty frames back into the wrappings and turned to leave, the seedy-looking gent stepped into the room, picked up the parcel and said, "Excuse me gov'nor, but I just bought these from t'e missus. I collect old frames." With that he turned and left. We stepped outside to see him quickly drive down the street.

Before I could speak, Aunt Harri said, "Would you believe that man insisted on paying me $100 for those old picture frames. I'd have taken $10 for the lot." Feeling sick, I wished Aunt Harri good luck, and forgetting the small pile of books I had set aside, we headed home.

Inside I remembered the books, three Costain novels that

would have completed my collection, but I couldn't return—
would remind me of the loss of a genuine Krieghoff.

That evening after Aunt Harri and Margo had cleared up,
the tired oldster carrying a shopping bag came over to share
our evening meal.

"Did things go well" I asked.

"Yes pretty good. Didn't like those dealers who arrived
early. Got my own back though. Got thinking about the chap
who paid too much for the picture frames and figured out
what happened. I'm sure he saw an old Krieghoff print,
couldn't tell it from the real thing in the dark room, and
bought it quickly before anyone else could."

I just gulped; I couldn't speak.

Aunt Harri continued, "Nothing worse than greed to drive
a person. Oh, thought you would like these. You folks have
been such a great help to me."

With that, she pulled three Costain novels from her bag.

Aunt Harri Embarks on a New Adventure

I recognized Aunt Harri's faltering handwriting on the letter
that arrived in my mailbox just days after she had moved to
Village Mews seniors' home. We missed her daily visits. I
quickly opened the envelope to share the contents with Anna.
As I read the following words, I noticed that Aunt Harri, who
often spoke in clipped English, wrote with an even flow.

Dear Friends:

I appreciated your help during my last few days, and for
your offer to drive me here. Sorry that I had to say no. I

made the decision to come here, so I felt I must come alone. The taxi driver carried in my trunk and suitcase and left me standing just inside the lobby.

I looked down the long corridor toward the office and nursing station and said to myself, "Dear God, what have I done?" For a few moments I didn't know what to do. Then suddenly the years dropped away and I saw myself standing on the dock in Liverpool waiting to board a ship to Canada to start a new life. I had all my possessions in an old steamer trunk and my WAAC's duffle bag. I had felt young and lonely even though many other travellers and shipping employees crowded the dock. I clearly heard the sound of ships' horns and bells, and workmen labouring to get everything on board. I had said exactly the same thing then, wondering if I had made a complete fool of myself by deciding to emigrate, and wondering how I would ever get my things to my cabin.

Rather suddenly, a persistent ship's bell crowded into my thoughts. A young woman dressed in a white uniform stepped up to me and said, "You must be Mrs. Brown. Welcome to Village Mews. That's the lunch bell, but we have time to show you to your room." It took me a moment to come back over the 70 plus years, to leave the dock, the confusion, and the ship and adjust to the nursing home. I muttered a muddled yes to the young woman as she picked up my bag. She told me someone else would get my trunk and then guided me down the long hallway.

We entered a bright room with two beds. The young woman explained that Mrs. Marshall would join me in a day or two. I must have been a little confused still for I looked out the window and asked, "Is this cabin on the port or starboard side?"

She took me to the dining hall where I met my table mates. We always eat at the same table so we can get to know a few folk fairly well. Later I found my way back to my

room and sat in a comfortable chair near my trunk, intending
to read the "Welcome to Village Mews" booklet I had found
in the room. Then I eyed the second bed and again questioned
my judgment. Why would anyone commit herself to moving
in with a perfect stranger?

Then I remembered clutching a wad of letters in my hand
as I sat at the window of a transcontinental train. Black smoke
and soot drifting past the window clouded my vision while
the rattle of wheels on tracks and the hissing and puffing of
the steam engine assaulted my ears. As woods, lakes, and then
prairie passed the window I read and reread the letters. Again
and again I said to myself, "Harri, you've done a fool thing
this time. You're going to Alberta to marry a man you met
only once. You know him from his letters alone. In a few
days you will not only occupy the same room, but the same
bed!"

Just then the door of my compartment opened and a
conductor stepped in. I tried to hide the letters by dropping
them beside my seat. As the conductor approached, his
uniform turned from blue to white. In fact he became a she,
who said, "Hello Mrs. Brown, I'm the duty nurse, we need to
talk about your medication." Then she bent down to retrieve
the booklet I had dropped.

Yes, moving in here has been a bit worrisome. But when
I think about it, it's no different than a dozen other trips and
adventures I have had throughout my life.

Do come and see me in a week or two when I get settled.
Best Wishes,
Aunt Harri

I looked at Anna and said, "I think Aunt Harri will do
just fine. When you've had over 90 years of experience, you
can handle almost anything."

An Unhappy Camper

The first time we visited Aunt Harri at Village Mews, we found her alone in a small lounge not far from her room. She sat in a chair looking straight ahead, her right hand resting on the top of her ever-present cane, her mouth a straight line, and a book unopened on her lap. I had never seen her look so old and tired.

"I am not happy here," she declared. "I may have made another foolish mistake. They have put me in with another woman I just can't live with. They won't have a private room for about a month."

"Exactly what's wrong?" I asked.

"The other woman is blind. Because she can't see, she has a clock that chimes every hour. She snores loudly and doesn't sleep well. When she wakes in the night she turns on her radio. I have not slept since I moved here. When I complain to her, she says, 'Yes, dear,' but doesn't do anything about it. It's like talking to a stone wall. She is a thoughtless, ignorant, old woman."

"Have you talked to the administrator?" I inquired.

"Yes. She doesn't understand. When my son comes next week, I will ask him to speak to her."

I looked at Aunt Harri's tired features, thinking she might not last another week. "Do you mind if I speak to her?" I asked.

"If you don't mind. It might help."

I headed for the administrator's office wondering how I could help. Aunt Harri acts more assertively than I do. Not liking confrontations, I steeled myself as I entered the office. The lady in charge greeted me and I defined the problem.

She assumed an authoritative pose and proceeded to explain the facts of life to me. "Older folks" she said, "when they have lived alone, find it difficult to adjust to others. The habits and attitudes of strangers bother them. It often takes a few weeks to adjust. Mrs. Harriet Brown has requested a private room, but it won't be convenient to arrange that for a few weeks. Even then, she will have to share a bathroom with a woman in an adjacent room. I'm sure she will complain about the toilet flushing and about the other lady using her towel."

"But," I insisted, "Mrs. Brown isn't sleeping well, the other lady . . ."

"Mrs. Brown will get used to the snoring. I am sure she will be fine in a day or two."

I tried again, "But in a private room . . ."

"I have explained that moving her wouldn't be convenient for a few weeks, and wouldn't likely help anyway," cut in the administrator. With that she stood to her feet to dismiss me.

To myself I said, "Time to get tough Ray. Put on an irate consumer act." I raised my hand, palm outward, like a policeman giving a stop command. I furrowed my brow and forced the edges of my mouth downward. I gave no indication of moving from my chair. The hard-hearted administrator gave me a startled look and sat down.

"Mrs. Brown is paying you good money to stay here," I said, trying to project anger in my voice. "If you can't give her good service, then we will find another home for her. If she cannot sleep at night, she will become dreadfully ill, or even die. I will speak to her about moving immediately."

"But you won't find a better or cheaper place than this," stammered the administrator.

"Price is not the issue," I said as I rose, spun on my heel, and marched out.

I reported back to Aunt Harri, who said, "Let's give it a few more days."

I left in an angry mood: angry with the aging process, angry with our society that tolerates institutional living for old folks, angry with the administrator for her callous attitude, and angry with myself for my phony masquerade.

Two days later we again visited Aunt Harri. She sat in the same chair waiting for us with a radiant look on her face. The Aunt Harri we knew and loved had returned. "An amazing, thing happened," she said. "The afternoon you visited, they moved me into a private room. I can sleep. The administrator has visited me every day to see how I'm doing. You must meet my new friend, who eats at my table, Mrs. Louise Clayton. This is a good place!"

A Place Among the Relics

One glorious Saturday last summer, we offered to take Aunt Harri to the grocery store. As we drove toward town on the county road, we caught up to five or six slow-moving cars. At the head of the pack I could see the outline of an ancient car. One by one the traffic scooted past it until nothing but empty pavement separated us from a Model-T Ford roadster.

The driver and passenger sat bolt upright: protected from the breeze by a high windshield and shielded from the sun by a black canvas top. Their clothing and an auto rug pulled over their legs flapped as air rushed around the windshield and buffeted them. Aunt Harri leaned forward from the rear seat to watch the black antique. "Open your window," she commanded.

I have learned to obey Aunt Harri's orders. The open window clearly brought the sound of the Model-T to us. The steady beat of the ancient engine, coupled with the rush of air transported us in our imaginations back 70 years to the days when driving was high adventure. I checked my speedometer: 52 kilometres per hour, about 33 miles per hour. "Can you believe that," I exclaimed, "he's running at full throttle!"

At the edge of town the Ford slowed, the driver gave an arm signal, and swung left into the grounds of the recreation centre. Only then did we notice a line of old cars preparing to leave. We stopped to watch. The Model-T joined the end of the parade and followed along as 20 or more elderly machines headed into town.

"Follow them," Aunt Harri insisted. We tagged along until the wheeled antiques turned into the museum and pulled up in neat rows.

"Drop me off here, while you park," Aunt Harri instructed. She got briskly from the car and made a beeline for a huge, old limousine, painted deep maroon. When we got back to her she stood with her cane braced on the running board of the big car, staring into the driver's compartment.

"It's an old Lincoln," she said, turning toward us. "The owner told me it belonged to Ned Sparks. Left it in Toronto during the war when he couldn't get gas to drive back to the States."

"What drew you to this car?" I asked. "Did you once own one like it?" Without answering, Aunt Harri walked to a picnic table and sat down where she had a good view of the Lincoln. We sat beside her.

"Didn't own one. But for a minute it was like seeing an old friend from 70 years ago. The car I remember was a 1926 Willys Knight—about the size and shape of that one." She sat silently, until I prodded her to go on.

"My boss, a factory owner, had it; drove it himself. I worked for him in his home as cook in the '20s when he ran a plant in London. In the summer he would drive us—me, a maid, and the Chinese houseboy—to his summer home on the St. Clair River. Called the place OK Corunna. We would go down early and open the place up so he could bring his family a few days later."

Again Aunt Harri became silent for a few moments as though staring into the past. She continued: "I'll never forget one trip. We headed out on the road people called the Sarnia Gravel with me in the back with the maid and the houseboy beside the boss in front. The big car ran very quietly—people called that model the 'Silent Knight.' Had a special engine. He called it a sleeve-valve engine. You could always recognize one by the blue smoke trailing behind it. Anyway when he got it up to 80 miles an hour the houseboy turned to us with eyes as big as saucers and said, 'Oh, look, look, lookie, 80!' The boss used to scare the daylights out of all three of us. Never had an accident. Though I must confess I nearly messed my britches a time or two."

Aunt Harri paused again, and stared up and down the rows of old cars, the Lincoln, a number of Model-Ts and Model-As, an old Dodge station wagon, a Hillman, and a variety of others. She spoke again, "Funny how young people enjoy fixing up these old relics of the past, but rarely bother with us old folks who are the real relics of another time. We owned these things. They're part of our lives. We could tell true stories about every one, and about a lot of other things, if someone would just ask us."

The Case of the
Disappearing Dentures

When Anna and I dropped in on Aunt Harri at Village Mews we found her sitting alone in the lobby watching rain spattering on the front windows and lightning arcing through the black overhanging clouds. We greeted her as we dropped into chairs, one on each side of her.

"Nice display of God's handiwork," she said as a bright bolt split the heavens.

I waited for the thunderclap to echo its last, then said, "Yes, it's like having a front-row seat on judgment day. Do you often sit here and watch the weather?"

"Sometimes. Because of my failing sight, I can't read for long, and I can't watch television, so this makes a pleasant change."

"How do you spend your time?" Anna asked.

Another flash of lightning and crack of thunder delayed Aunt Harri's answer: "I read as much as I can. Walk around the building, or chat with the other folks here. Sometimes I just sit and think. Today, before the storm started, I was thinking about teeth."

"Teeth?" I questioned.

"False teeth. Lower dentures," she answered. "I have false teeth—lowers."

"I didn't realize you had dentures," Anna remarked.

"That's because I keep them in my mouth, unlike Mr. Nolan who nearly lost his last week. Did you know that I once fitted my own false teeth?"

I wondered how Nolan lost his teeth, but said, "Explain yourself. How did you fit your own teeth?"

"On the farm in Alberta in the early forties, I couldn't get to a dentist in Edmonton when I broke my lower plate. In those days, when we needed something that the general store couldn't provide we ordered it from Eaton's catalogue. So I got my new teeth by mail order."

"You got false teeth from Eaton's catalogue?" Anna asked incredulously.

"Oh no," Aunt Harri laughed "from a dental company. They sent me a kit containing a wax form or mouthpiece. I heated the wax and bit into it leaving the impression of my gums. I sent that back to the company, they made my new teeth, and mailed them back. They fitted perfectly. I wore them for years."

"What has that to do with Mr. Nolan's teeth?" I asked.

"Nothing. Mr. Nolan's teeth just reminded me how I used to fit my own. He sits to my right at the table. He has the disgusting habit of removing his teeth when he eats and putting them on his bread-and-butter plate."

I interrupted, "I thought people wore false teeth so they could eat properly. Why does he take them out?"

"He says they hurt his mouth. I guess he wears them for looks. Anyway, he takes them out when he needs to chew his main course, and usually leaves them in for soup and desserts. He pops them out and puts the disgusting things right next to my teacup. Maybe it's a blessing my eyes aren't as good as they used to be."

"Last week the soup was very hot so Mr. Nolan put it to his left to cool. Then as usual he removed his denture to eat his meat and potatoes. As he finished his main course and reached for his soup, a waitress removed the dirty dishes. Nolan also reached for his teeth, but they were gone. Did he get mad! He caused a terrible uproar, bawled out the waitress, and ordered the kitchen staff to search till they found his missing teeth.

"I suggested he eat his soup before it got cold. Let the staff search the dishwasher and garbage can for the lost chompers. He dipped his spoon into the soup, but started yelling again when he found a foreign object in it. The waitress still shaking from the last encounter came to look. She used Nolan's soup spoon to fish the object out, then gleefully held up the lost denture. Nolan turned beet red, but never said a word."

"How," I asked, "did the teeth get in the soup?"

Aunt Harri waited for another thunderclap to subside, turned her eyes heavenward and answered, "Some parts of a story are best forgotten to protect the guilty."

Aunt Harri Belts a Driver

Aunt Harri raised her cane shoulder high, yelled like a cow moose protecting its calf, and charged the blue van. I remember freezing on the spot . . . but I had better tell the whole story.

About a year before Aunt Harri's eyesight began to deteriorate, we took her on a shopping trip to the city. She settled into the back seat and began fiddling with the seat belt. When I offered to help, she rather crustily said, "I'm quite capable, thank you."

As she snapped the belt together, I said, "Seat belts are a nuisance."

"Yes. But only an old fool would drive without one. When you get old and brittle like me, even minor accidents kill," Aunt Harri opined.

As I slid behind the wheel, I asked. "Do you think belts are only for old people?"

"There are just as many young fools as old fools. Old people don't like change. They argue that they got through 60 or 80 years without seat belts and don't need them now."

Aunt Harri sat quietly in thought until we reached the highway, then volunteered: "Had a bad accident once. Hit a big car head on at 55 miles per hour. My son was driving. I heard him yell, 'I can't miss! I can't miss!.' Next thing I knew people were pulling us out of the car. My oldest son, riding in what we used to call the death seat, got concussion and a fractured pelvis. The rest of us got serious bruises. Spent two weeks in hospital. That happened long before cars had seat belts. Belts would have saved us."

At the mall, we went our separate ways, meeting at the

food court at four o'clock. "No coffee for me," said Aunt
Harri. "I get snarly when I drink it late in the day."

As Anna and I drank our decaf and Aunt Harri sipped
apple juice, we watched the passing parade. One young family
caught our attention. A red-faced, overweight man marched
along ahead of a thin, tired-looking woman. She led a toddler
by the hand and pushed another in a stroller. Two boys, about
eight and nine brought up the rear. The oldest boy looked like
a miniature of his father. The younger boy and the woman
struggled with parcels. He carried one under each arm; she
balanced two on the stroller.

The procession stopped directly in front of us. "Meet us
at the south door in 20 minutes," Red Face ordered the
woman. With that he and his mini-clone departed.

As the woman began moving, both parcels fell from the
stroller. I jumped up and helped reload them. With a timid
voice she said, "Thank you," and led her brood southward.

Forty minutes later, Anna, Aunt Harri, and I left by the
south door. Surprised, we saw the family waiting patiently
and silently at the curb. As we watched a blue van pulled up
in front of them. Red Face sat at the wheel with his clone
beside him. The clone, kneeling on the front seat, faced the
rear playing with a yoyo.

The woman opened the side door and loaded the kids and
parcels before turning her attention to the stroller. After a
two-minute struggle she folded it and climbed in, getting at
least one good bop on the head from the clone's yoyo. She
closed the door as Red Face looked back to check traffic.

Right then Aunt Harri made her move. As Red Face
began to engage the clutch, he heard the animal cry and
looked forward to see an angry, elderly woman blocking his
way. She stood with one hand on the van's snub nose and
wielded her cane with the other. She struck the windshield
three times, then moved to the driver's door, giving it a
resounding whack.

"Don't you dare!" Aunt Harri yelled into the driver's face, and pointed the business end of her cane at the mini-clone. "Don't you dare move this car until you make that child sit down and fasten his seat belt. How dare you risk the lives of your family?"

Red Face blushed deeper crimson, fastened his and his son's belt and drove off without a word. Aunt Harri walked slowly to our car.

"You could have been killed," I chided when I caught up.

"Pooh," she answered. "It takes a feisty old lady with a cane to put fear into them."

As we carefully belted ourselves in, I turned to Anna and asked, "How would she act with a coffee or two under her belt?"

Aunt Harri Shares the Whole Picture

Aunt Harri came to visit one weekend, bringing a small, grey, shoe box. From the illustration and price tag on the end of the box, I deduced she had owned it for many years—decades have passed since you could buy ankle-length, button-up, dress shoes for $3.95. Across the top in a firm British hand, I read the words: "Personal property of Harriet Brown."

Aunt Harri saw me eyeing the box, and curtly said, "Personal, like it says. Show you tomorrow, if you're interested."

I forgot about the box until next day when Aunt Harri brought it to the lunch table; again I gave it a curious stare. She patted it gently on the lid and said, "Don't worry, it's Harriet's box, not Pandora's. I'll open it after lunch."

After finishing a slice of Anna's delicious no-crust
pumpkin pie, Aunt Harri commanded, "Clear the table and I
will open the box. This old box is my storehouse of
memories. I brought it so you could help me restore some old
adventures and put new life into some precious moments."

Not sure what the box contained or what she expected of
me, but bursting with curiosity, I said, "Open the thing!"

Just as Anna cleared the last dish, Aunt Harri removed
the lid and tipped the box. Hundreds of pictures spilled onto
the table: old portraits in leather folders; postcard-sized shots
of men and women in uniform and military equipment; box
Brownie pictures of people, farms, beaches, horses, and old
cars with families posed about them. As Aunt Harri fanned
them out, I saw scenes of a serious young woman in a
WAAC uniform, a happy young person in 1920s beachwear
and on the deck of an ocean liner, a slightly older woman on
a farm with children about her, and a middle-aged woman
standing in front of a 1951 Austin.

"Memories, all of them," said Aunt Harri. "I want you to
help me with them, to help me select some of the best and
arrange them, because you know about things like that."

I still didn't know what she wanted, or what she thought
I knew about, but I waited, knowing she would tell me in
good time.

Deftly Aunt Harri began sifting through the pile,
sometimes squinting at individual pictures with her troubled
eyes, but mostly identifying them by feel. Some she caressed
gently before placing them aside; some brought a twinkle to
her eyes; one triggered a frown; many inspired an outright
smile or chuckle. Once she paused for a long time, carefully
studying a sepia print. When she gently laid it aside I saw a
tear stain on one corner of the photo showing an older man
with a wide-brimmed hat posed in a field of grain.

We sat in silence for many minutes watching Aunt
Harri's performance. When she finally looked up she had

separated out five piles of photos with three to six in each pile. She carefully packed the rest in the box and replaced the lid. Next, she picked up one pile and fanned it out before us. "Pictures of my husband and I before we met," she said simply.

I saw photos of a handsome young man: one in a military uniform; another showed the same man seated with others in battle dress before a tent; a third placed him astride a racing bicycle. Three more revealed a young woman: first in a World War I WAAC uniform; next on the deck of an ocean liner; lastly working with a group of laughing women in a candy factory.

"These will go along the top. The next pictures from my married life on the farm will go next, and so on." She finally pointed to a collection showing an aging Aunt Harri. "These will go along the bottom to complete it." Having finished her explanation, she sat back with a far-away look.

"Along the top and bottom of what?" I asked, still in the dark.

"Oh, I'm sorry," said Aunt Harri, coming back to the present. I want you to take these to your friend Jim, the photographer. Get him to make a large collage with them, and make 11 copies of it. I want to frame the collages and give one to each of my children and grandchildren as Christmas presents."

After a pause, she said, "Memories are for sharing, not hiding in an old shoe box."

Tess Spans the Generation Gap

We had promised to take 12-year-old Tess to a children's
movie. Tess comes from an underprivileged, single parent
home. She always seems so sad, rarely smiling. I don't
remember ever hearing her laugh. We thought a good
children's movie might bring a smile to her face. Truthfully,
we like children's movies ourselves and feel embarrassed
when we go without a child.

As an afterthought we asked Aunt Harri to come along.
We had Tess on board when we picked up our older friend at
Village Mews. We introduced them and saw the instant bond
that often occurs between the very young and the very old. As
we pulled onto the highway, Aunt Harri began a conversation
that held us spellbound for the rest of the trip. I actually
drove slowly, just to extend the magic.

"That's a beautiful coat," said Aunt Harri to Tess. "Did
you get it for Christmas?"

Tess beamed and nodded. Through the rear-view mirror I
noticed Aunt Harri run her hand over the quality material and
stop momentarily at a button that didn't quite match the
others.

"It really is lovely, I am glad you can still get that style.
Did your mother give it to you?"

"No, I don't have a . . . my father gave it to me."

From Aunt Harri's next words, I realized she had grasped
the significance of the "pre-worn" coat and Tess's hesitant
answer. She said, "God has blessed you with a father who can
buy you special things. My children grew up without a father.
My husband took ill when they were little and stayed in
hospital till he died. I couldn't get them nice things like your

new coat. They had to wear hand-me-downs from the
neighbour's older kids. I made some things for them from
sugar and flour sacks. I knitted all their socks and gloves
from used wool I unravelled from old sweaters. They were
lucky kids."

"Lucky? How could kids like that be lucky," demanded
Tess.

"Well," said Aunt Harri. "They had one parent to look
after them; some kids have none. They had neighbours who
shared. They didn't freeze to death in the winter, and we had
lots to eat because we grew our own vegetables."

"Why might they freeze to death? Did you live in
Siberia?" asked Tess with a growing brightness in her voice.

"Almost," laughed Aunt Harri. "We lived on the Canadian
prairies. We didn't have enough coal to warm the whole
house, so the boys slept upstairs with very little heat. They
had to break the ice in the basin to wash their faces and clean
their teeth."

Another glance in the rear-view mirror showed Tess with
a look of disbelief on her face as she asked, "Didn't the water
pipes and the toilet freeze?"

"Didn't have any pipes. We got the water from a well.
No toilet either. We used an outside privy. If the kids took
too long doing their business, I had to treat their bottoms for
frostbite."

Both Aunt Harri and Tess doubled up with laughter. It
took Tess a few moments before she could ask another
question—this time a deadly serious one: "Aunt Harri, my
school counsellor told me that kids who grow up in difficult
homes have problems when they grow up. I feel sorry for
your family."

"Well don't. They turned into well-adjusted adults. Kids
who grow up fighting the cold, working in the garden, and
carrying water from the well in midwinter grow up into
tough, independent people. They can handle most problems

that come their way. They certainly didn't grow up to become pains in the butt like some kids I have known."

Tess looked at Aunt Harri with real respect on her face, but suddenly dissolved into laughter.

Puzzled, Aunt Harri said, "Now young lady, what brought on that display of hilarity. I don't think I said anything funny."

Tess answered between staccato bursts of laughter: "It's just that I thought they couldn't possibly grow up to be pains in the butt if they had got their backsides frozen off in an outdoor toilet!"

Ray and Anna Climb the Tower

Some days we get ourselves into the dumbest situations and don't know how to get out. Last spring we did it again when we offered to take Aunt Harri to Niagara Falls.

All morning we tramped around the small shops—even spent some time in two of the museums. Aunt Harri insisted we go to Tussaud's. Apparently Madame Tussaud's had been a favourite spot of hers in Old London sometime between the wars. Before lunch we stood along the railing looking at the falls, while Aunt Harri regaled us with stories from her memory: stories about Blondin and his wheelbarrow, and about people who had gone over in barrels. Most of the events she described happened over 60 years ago. When lunch time arrived, I suggested we head for the car and go find a restaurant.

"Oh, no," Aunt Harri insisted. "I know of a little English tearoom near here. We can walk there."

Concerned that Aunt Harri would tire herself, I said, "We better drive, even if it is near."

"Phooey, you young folks have forgotten how to walk," Aunt Harri snorted, taking off at an army pace.

We had no choice but follow behind.

We walked and walked, around and around, passing one corner three times. It seemed obvious to me that Aunt Harri had forgotten the tearoom's location. Finally she stopped, tapped her cane against the wall of a craft store, and said, "It was right here."

"When were you last in it?" asked Anna.

"Oh, just in," Aunt Harri began, but hesitated in embarrassment. ". . . in 1959. I guess it could have closed by now."

I went for the car, picked up Aunt Harri and Anna, and took them to a family restaurant. As we ate, I noticed Aunt Harri had become very quiet. I assumed she felt chagrined over the English tearoom, or maybe she had just worn herself out. I suggested we drive to Queenston Heights. I wanted to slow the old girl down and get a chance to relax myself.

We all agreed, so one hour later found us seated on a bench looking toward the Brock monument. Anna had brought her binoculars, so she amused herself looking at birds and distant scenery.

When Aunt Harri finally spoke, I realized the incident of the English tearoom still bothered her: "Getting older is like looking backwards with a telescope. Everything is there, especially the events of long ago. The near things appear hazy; sometimes you don't see them at all."

Suddenly, Aunt Harri stood up. "That's the Brock monument," she said. "I think I'll climb it." With that she took off across the grass straight toward the tower.

Anna and I caught up and did our best to convince her not to even think of climbing the monument, but to no avail. Aunt Harri just lectured us: "I am in good shape for my age. If you young folk can't handle it, wait for me at the bottom. I don't like people saying I'm too old to do what others do."

As we neared the tower, Anna and I felt desperate; if we

had brought a rope we would have hog-tied the oldster. With just yards to go, Aunt Harri stopped, pointed to a bench, and said, "You two go ahead; I'll wait here."

We felt so much relief we quit thinking. We just walked around to the entrance and climbed to the top. Even "young folks" like us in their 60s shouldn't climb towers. On the way back down I called out to Anna speeding on ahead of me, "I think we have been had."

When we rounded the tower, we saw Aunt Harri in conversation with an elderly man sitting on the same bench. The old chap must have had poor hearing for Aunt Harri spoke loudly enough for us to hear, "As you grow older, never let the younger generation think you're slipping. It doesn't matter that you can't do everything you once did. What matters is that you convince them you can do everything they can."

Hurricane Harri Hits Village Mews

Anna and I called for Aunt Harri one stormy winter day. Black clouds hung low on the horizon, and a chill wind blew from the north. We had promised to take the spunky oldster to the city for a shopping trip.

As we entered Village Mews, we sensed another storm. Two nurses stood at their station staring down the hallway. They spoke in low voices, stopping abruptly as we drew near. Further along the passage we passed the open door of a sitting room. Inside a group of older women chatted in loud voices, not caring who heard. One voice said, "She certainly made them pay attention. Now maybe they will do something about that young pill pusher." A second voice answered, "I think she overreacted. The doctor just has his job to do. Don't go on so just because he's young."

"Job my foot," returned the first voice. "No doctor should treat people as if nothing matters just because they are old. If he talks to you at all, he talks down to you as if you still wore diapers."

A third voice, crackling with laughter, said, "Don't forget dearie, some of us do wear diapers."

We passed by.

Further along, we neared two men leaning on canes. The tall one with the walnut cane said, "Never saw anything so funny in all my life. I heard the ruckus, stepped out of my room, and the pill pusher came storming out of her room as though the devil had him by the coattails."

The short one with the white cane said, "I heard her yelling. Well not really yelling. Let's say she used that big, powerful voice of hers effectively. She bellowed like an army sergeant: 'Don't you ever enter my room again, you insensitive young quack.'"

Both men chuckled together as we eased past and continued toward Aunt Harri's room. On the right side, three doors stood open. In each doorway, stood a senior: two ladies in dressing gowns, and a man with a walker. Each looked at a closed door across the way—Aunt Harri's room. A statuesque nurse in a smartly starched uniform stood at Aunt Harri's door, as though on guard.

Alarmed, we rushed forward. The nurse smiled, then said in a deep, refined, Caribbean accent, "Don't worry. Mrs. Brown is okay. The superintendent is with her. Give them a moment."

A moment later the door opened and the superintendent came out. She nodded. I thought I saw a discerning smile. We entered to see Aunt Harri in her recliner. I imagined a small, black storm-cloud hovering over her head.

She saw us enter, and brightened noticeably. "Morning," she said, "Don't think I should go out today. Too stormy. Both inside and out."

"What is wrong?" asked Anna.

"Nothing now. Things have just started to go right. I just dismissed my doctor—not really my doctor, the home's doctor."

"What happened," I asked.

"My heart started to race a month or two ago. He gave me some medicine. Never told me anything; never explained what was wrong; never told me about side effects. Nothing. I tried to ask, but he was too busy, and hurried away. A few days later I started getting shortness of breath. Couldn't even walk to the dining room without resting. The next week the doctor gave me more pills. He said they would overcome the shortness of breath."

"What did he say was wrong?" asked Anna.

"He didn't say. Just treated me like a senile cast-off. I just wanted to know what was wrong. Would I have to live with the problem? Can something be done? If I knew, I could adjust my life accordingly. So today I fired him. I think Village Mews will too."

"But what about your health?" I asked.

By now Aunt Harri had recovered her sense of humour. "I'm all right," she said. "I went back to my old doctor three days ago. He said I suffered mostly from side effects, so he took me off all medication except one new pill for the racing heart. Said I had another century in me."

Aunt Harri chuckled for a moment, then said, "Yes, I'm my old self again—as my neighbours will tell you."

Aunt Harri Reflects on the Simple Life

On a bright spring day we took Aunt Harri on an outing to the picturesque village of St. Jacobs. She quickly wore us out visiting the shops, so we looked for a diversion—something to slow her down. We found it in the Meeting Place, a museum that portrays the roots, history, and religious practices of the Mennonite people who settled and still live in the St. Jacobs' area. Aunt Harri indeed slowed down; her mood became serious and contemplative. She said very little.

As we left the Meeting Place, we realized the bright sun had disappeared behind angry forbidding clouds; drops of rain sent us scurrying for the car. In minutes we had left the village and started for home over a network of county roads. Suddenly the spattering rain turned to cloudburst. I eased the car onto the shoulder, turned on the four-way flashers, stopped the engine, and prepared to wait it out. In about five minutes the downpour eased enough to see the road again, so I re-started the car and prepared to pull out.

Glancing back over my shoulder to check for traffic, I saw a dark image moving quickly toward us. If it made any noise as it hurtled past, the drumming rain on our roof drowned it out. I suppose it remained in view for only a few seconds, but it impressed a vivid picture on our minds before disappearing into the storm.

An ebony horse had emerged from the murk behind us, its shiny, wet coat reflecting glitters of red from our car's taillights. With its head held high but forward, its nose pointed straight into the storm. Its legs, moving with the smoothness of a sulky pacer, seemed to spin like great wheels, throwing up a thick mist of water. As it shot past only an

arm's length from the car window, I visualized the powerful
legs as drive wheels on a steam locomotive. The image
appeared so real I fully expected the cars of an express train
to follow.

Instead I saw the black body of a buggy or democrat.
Crouching low in the front seat, a young man wearing clothes
as black as the horse and carriage held the reins. His face, wet
and glistening in the glare of our taillights, radiated sheer
adventure. Beside him a woman, her dark skirts wrapped
tightly around her legs, further protected herself from the
driving rain with an umbrella. As the wind buffeted the
umbrella, I glimpsed a young, beautiful, laughing face.

In a moment they had gone, disappearing into the
blackness of another squall.

I made no attempt to drive on, but just sat there for a
moment before saying, "Wow!"

Anna said nothing, but Aunt Harri finally spoke from the
back seat: "That and the visit to the Meeting Place sure
carried me back."

The rain continued, so we drove slowly back to the
village and took refuge in the Stone Crock restaurant. Seated
at a table with heaps of Mennonite cooking before us, I said
to Aunt Harri, "Earlier you said something about being carried
back. I didn't know you were a Mennonite."

"I'm not—well maybe partly. In Alberta back in the '30s
and '40s the local village had only one Protestant church—
Mennonite. We attended it; my children went to Sunday
school there; they buried my husband from that church. The
people were wonderful, only a few came from Mennonite
backgrounds, and they considered themselves progressive."

"Did they drive cars or buggies?" I asked.

"Mostly buggies and wagons, because only a few could
afford cars back then. We drove a buggy almost everywhere
in summer and a cutter or closed van in the winter. We put
up with heat in summer, cold in winter, and gumbo in spring.

Yes, we too raced the rain and, sometimes, the prairie dust storms."

"Do you ever want to go back to those times?" asked Anna.

"Sure, we all do at times, but we can't. It helps to know that some people still live that way, close to the land, close to nature, close to God, and oft times on the sheer edge of fun and adventure."

An Enemy Crouches at the Door

As we approached Aunt Harri's door, we could hear the sound of an audio book playing. The click of the stop button and a sharp call from Aunt Harri signalled us to come in. As we entered, she turned on the light.

"Can't read much now so talking books help keep the prime enemy of the aged at bay," said Aunt Harri from the recliner in her room at Village Mews.

"The prime enemy?" I asked.

"Yes, he is there, crouching at the door, skulking in dark places, and patrolling the hallways. Like most older folk, I fear him more than the ghostly rider on the pale horse."

"Aunt Harri, you have become so poetic, so literary, I don't know what you're talking about," I said.

"Loneliness," she answered.

We didn't respond. What can you say to someone in her nineties, sitting alone in the dark, listening to a canned voice reading an adventure thriller.

"At least I spent my life getting toughened up to deal with loneliness. It first found me as a child when Mother died. A little girl especially needs a mother. Then I joined the WAACS and went to France in the Great War. There loneliness weighted me down worse than my army greatcoat in summertime. Had lots of friends, young laughing friends, but you can't feel more alone and afraid than while cowering in a dugout with bombs exploding outside, dirt falling from the roof, and crying girls all around. Experiences like that make even young people hard and tough."

Aunt Harri paused, her nearly-blind eyes staring far back into the past. We waited quietly.

"Then I came to Canada, alone and ill," Aunt Harri continued. "I feared loneliness. I didn't want to be alone when the thunder clapped or a car backfired and I collapsed trembling and shaking. Shellshock, they called it. At the same time I didn't want people seeing me like that. At that time some dear friends took an interest in me. In a little gospel hall, I had a spiritual rebirth, I met the Lord. After that, loneliness never held me so tightly."

Aunt Harri awkwardly wiped her eyes with the back of her hand before picking up the story again: "Then I moved to Alberta. Got married and the strain of loneliness fled. Except when Fred had business away from the farm and a fearful prairie dust storm struck. The sun went dark and the old frame house shook and danced on its foundation. I would pray that God would send Fred home quickly—and he would come, driving the white team at breakneck speed through the blackness because he understood my fear."

Aunt Harri paused to rest her voice. I could think of nothing to say, but she broke the silence: "We went to England, came back to Canada, then Fred took ill—six years and three kids later. They took him to the provincial mental hospital—a place called Ponoka. Loneliness again tried to crush me, but I didn't let it. Now there were three depending on me, so I fought back. We fought more than loneliness, we stood with our backs to the wall, we fought off poverty, and we wrestled with bureaucracy. And together we won."

Aunt Harri took a sip of water, blew her nose and took us

to the next chapter: "Then the kids grew up and moved on into their own lives. The old enemy tried to return, but I made new friends, travelled, visited with my grandkids, and made myself useful in dozens of ways, and remained stubbornly independent. Then I came here. They put me in a room with a bed and a chair and a few of my treasures. And here I sit, always in the dark, nearly always alone, listening to a machine that reads to me."

Aunt Harri's sudden smile knocked me off balance. In confusion I blurted out: "Aunt Harri, if there is anything we can do . . ."

"Do!" she said. "You just did it. You visited me. You listened to me while I reminisced. You didn't interrupt. You let me babble on like this silly talking book. You let me go back and count God's blessing in my life. Thank you, and do come again—soon."

As we closed the door, we heard the light click off and the tape player re-start.

Slipping into the Twilight Zone

The call arrived at about 9:30 one evening: "I am calling from Village Mews. Mrs. Harriet Brown is very ill. She has slipped into a coma and we can't contact the family. Can you come?"

I started out immediately, leaving a note to explain my absence to Anna. When I arrived, they ushered me into Aunt Harri's room. The nurse said, "She had been deathly still until a few minutes ago. Now she is making noises and moving, almost as if she were dreaming."

Settling into a chair I took her aged hand in mine. She moved slightly and made a groaning sound. I spoke to her but got no response. I must have sat there for an hour in silence, then leaned forward resting my head on the bed, but still gripping Aunt Harri's hand. I realized she might not make it through the night, but if she wakened I wanted to be there.

I must have fallen asleep, for I found myself as an observer, not as a participant, in a bizarre dream. In my dream, two young women stood in the vestibule of a wooden railway car. The open upper half of the door looked out on lakes and woods rushing past. Smoke and ashes struck the side of the train forcing them to step back. I caught a glimpse of a black steam locomotive leaning into a sweeping curve between rocks and trees. The shorter of the women looked like a younger version of Aunt Harri. I overheard the taller one say, "You'll like Uncle Fred's farm in Alberta—he calls it a wheat ranch."

The scene changed. I watched the two leave the train in a prairie village. An older man and woman waiting on the platform spotted them. The man waved and said to his companion, "There's Dorothy and her friend."

"Hello Uncle Fred and Aunt Emily. Meet my friend Harriet," cried Dorothy. That scene faded out as the four piled into a Willys Overland touring car and drove along dusty, rutted roads.

Next I saw visions of Harriet and Dorothy riding in a buggy drawn by matched grays, picking wild flowers in a coulee bottom, riding on another pair of horses, trying to milk cows, and eating at a table piled high with food, while Fred and Emily played the perfect hosts.

A departure scene followed. On the wooden platform Dorothy and Harriet hugged Aunt Emily and Uncle Fred. The conductor yelled, "All 'board," as the engine hissed and whistled. The scene closed with a turmoil of steam, smoke, and noise.

I got momentary flashes of Harriet on the trip back east, arriving home, working in the kitchen of a grand house, singing before a church congregation, shopping in small stores, and opening a letter. Here the action slowed. From my observer's position, I read the letter over Harriet's shoulder. It said in old fashioned language: "Dear Harriet: Emily died a few months ago. I hope you don't think me bold for addressing this epistle to you. You see I am lonely and would like to correspond with you. . . . Sincerely, Fred."

More images flashed through my mind; pictures of Harriet receiving and sending letters. Eventually one arrived, saying, "Dearest Harri; Please marry me . . . "

Next followed scenes of excited shopping, of packing, of good-byes to Dorothy and others, and then a replay of the train trip, only with Harriet travelling alone in winter. I watched as Harriet caught sight of an 'Edmonton' sign, then excitedly gathered her things. Fred, looking handsome in a full suit with vest, waited on the platform with friends at his side. The next scenes blurred past quickly, then came into focus as Fred and Harriet holding hands stood before a justice of the peace. For the first time in this magical dream, I heard Harriet's voice. She said, "Yes Fred, I do. I love you Fred."

I not only saw Harriet's hand tighten on Fred's, I felt it! Awakened, I looked straight into Aunt Harri's open eyes. She spoke, "You're not my Fred. Why are you holding my hand?"

"You were dreaming, Aunt Harri; we were both dreaming," I said.

She looked puzzled: "Yes, my whole life was passing before me. I thought I was going."

Confused myself, I said, "You're not going anywhere. You're staying right here."

Aunt Harri Considers Birds, Flowers, and the Government

Just weeks after her near-death experience, Aunt Harri joined us for a walk in the woods.

Concerned about her health and medical care, I asked, "Do you worry about the lean and mean governments we have elected in recent years?"

Aunt Harri's mouth turned down and her lips pursed: "Worry about what?"

"About the decreasing health care available to older folk."

Aunt Harri's mind seemed to wander for she paused to look at an array of black-eyed Susans, pushing her cane into the ground like a gardener checking for moisture, then quoted, "Consider how the lilies grow. They neither labour nor spin. Yet not even Solomon was clothed like one of these."

She walked on a step or two then said, "My health is my problem. Never had any government looking after my health or the kids' either. In fact the only times the government got involved, the hardship increased."

"Did you have any medical emergencies when you lived on the farm?"

After carefully prodding a fallen tree trunk with her cane, Aunt Harri sat on it right next to an anthill. I sensed a story.

"When my daughter, Joy, was about three, I heard a scream and smelled burning flesh. Joy had fallen against a hot Quebec heater. Put her arms up to save herself. Didn't burn her face but seriously damaged her arms."

"Who did you call?" I unwisely asked.

"Didn't call anyone!" Aunt Harri thundered showing her

old energy and passion. "You couldn't call a soul from a snow-bound prairie farm in the forties. Had no man around, no phone, no car, not even a horse. When you faced an emergency, you didn't go whining to the government. You did the best you could."

"What did you do?" I asked.

"First aid. Rubbed Vaseline on the burns and bandaged them. Then I bundled up my oldest son and sent him to the nearest neighbour, a mile away. Neighbour arrived about two hours later in a van on sleighs to take us to the village a few miles away." As Aunt Harri talked she brushed her cane gently through a cluster of Queen Anne's lace.

"You went to a hospital?" I queried.

"No, to the doctor's office. And did he tell me off! Said I shouldn't have used Vaseline. Putting oil on a burn is the worst thing to do. Told me to use cold tea next time; it has tannic acid in it, a good treatment for burns. I shouldn't have bandaged her either. Thank God I didn't cause more serious problems. You can barely see the burn marks on her arms 50 years later."

"Did you have a medical plan of any sort?" I asked.

"Of course not! Paid the doctor what he asked, one dollar. Later gave him two fresh chickens," she replied before becoming silent.

Aunt Harri moved her attention to the ant hill. Her probing cane brought a flurry of activity, as the tiny creatures immediately began repairs to their home. She leaned forward so her aged eyes could better watch the action she had initiated. She posed a question: "Do they have a government to direct them, or do they just jump in and help each other to get the job done—like my neighbours on the farm?"

I said nothing, so Aunt Harri continued: "King Solomon said, 'Go to the ant, you sluggard; consider its ways and be wise.'"

I thought, "Her mind is wandering again."

As she stood to leave, a pair of frolicking goldfinches caught her attention. Again she quoted an ancient text: "Consider the ravens: they neither sow nor reap, yet God feeds them."

Aunt Harri said nothing more all the way back to the house. As she dropped into a chair on the porch, she suddenly blurted out: "Blast the government!"

Her out-of-character language startled me, making me think. I realized Aunt Harri's mind hadn't wandered back there in the woods. She had answered my questions by telling a story and drawing object lessons from nature—much like the Great Physician and Teacher had done 2000 years ago.

Aunt Harri Consults the Other Good Book

When Anna and I dropped in on Aunt Harri at Village Mews, we found her room empty. We hadn't seen her in the foyer where she often sits, so we headed for the nurse's station. "Has Mrs. Harriet Brown gone out for the day?" I asked.

"I don't believe so. Check the passage that joins the other building. She often sits there," answered the nurse.

The passage, lined with big windows, stretched about 20 metres between Aunt Harri's wing and the adjoining married couples' apartments. Chairs bordered each side, backs to the windows. We saw Aunt Harri about half way along, all alone. Her cane lay across the next chair, its handle just inches from her right hand. In her lap we could see a large open book with soft covers. Her left hand lay still on one page, while her right hand stroked slowly back and forth across the opposite page. Her eyes seem fixed on something far beyond the opposite windows.

As we drew near we could hear her quietly singing. Her deep voice, rich and vibrant despite her years, had an historic quality, like the sound of an early phonograph record: "I've been working on the railroad, all the live-long day . . ."

I had seen Aunt Harri in this trance-like mood before, so we turned and slipped quietly away, but not before we identified the book. Aunt Harri's hand was caressing a picture of a washing machine in the Sears Catalogue.

We visited the local doughnut shop for a half hour, then returned. We found Aunt Harri in the same chair, leafing through the catalogue. When she recognized us she removed her cane from the next chair. We sat one on each side of her.

"Doing some shopping?" I asked, pointing to the catalogue.

"No, I don't need anything. Just thinking, reminiscing," she answered quietly, a faraway tone creeping into her voice.

"With a Sears' catalogue?" I probed.

"Yes with a catalogue. Rather have an Eaton's, but they're long gone. Back on the farm the Eaton's catalogue was the second most important book. Brought a department store into the house. Bought my first washing machine from the catalogue."

"I thought you didn't have electric power," I interrupted.

"Didn't. It had a handle in the middle of the lid. The boys supplied the power. The wringer had a handle too. What a blessing to get rid of the scrubbing board. Also bought my cream separator from the catalogue. The boys also turned the handle on that. Got clothes and furniture too. We sang work songs while they swung the handle." Aunt Harri stared at the ceiling for a moment, then hummed a line of 'Working on the Railroad.'

"'Twas a dream book too. When the fall catalogue came, the kids spent hours studying it, dreaming about new toys, sleds, or toboggans. They'd make long lists. Most years we

could afford only one item for each child. I used it the same
way. I dreamed about new curtains, bright new wallpaper, an
indoor chemical closet, a comfortable chair. I longed to fill
my kids' wardrobes with clothes. I wanted new silver to
replace the stuff that had belonged to my husband's first wife.
I got very little of the extras—just the work things like the
washing machine. Still it was fun to open the catalogue and
escape into a never-never world of dreams."

Aunt Harri began to chuckle: "A farmer—bachelor,
lonely, not too bright, couldn't read—ordered a wife from the
catalogue. An unkind friend helped him fill out the order
form. Course all he got was a pretty red dress. Poor man was
too embarrassed to face anyone for over a year."

"So you were visiting that world of wishes and dreams
again," I said, picking up the catalogue.

"No. I was visiting the world most of us oldsters
enjoy—the world of memory, of things long past. The
catalogue with its bright shiny pages just helps me get there."

I looked at my watch and rose to leave. Aunt Harri gave
me a knowing smile and said, "Next time you come and find
me reminiscing, don't tippy-toe out. Sit down and wait a
minute or two till I turn the page of memories. I can come
back quickly for friends."

The Dirty Thirties and the Welfare State

Before moving from our country place into an apartment, we
invited Aunt Harri for a weekend. "Aunt Harri," I had said,
"We hope to sell, so it may be the last chance to visit your
old haunts."

We picked her up Saturday morning. Although Aunt
Harri displayed a quiet, contemplative mood, I felt the usual
rush of excitement. Something engaging always happens when
the whimsical nonagenarian puts in an appearance.

On Saturday evening we watched a videotape of a
National Film Board production entitled "The Drylanders,"
borrowed from the library. It follows the fortunes of turn-of-
the-century farmers who settled on Saskatchewan prairie. The
discouragements of a lost crop, life in a sod house, and
loneliness created tensions that would break most modern
marriages. But they survived, and things went well until the
Depression and nine-year drought of the 1930s. Some
abandoned their farms and returned to former homes or
moved to the Peace River district; a few remained.

Aunt Harri sat near the screen; this enabled her to see,
but put her in our line of sight. We saw tears running down
her cheeks when the farmer nearly died in a blizzard, when
the dust storms blew away the topsoil, and when families
abandoned their homes of 20 or 30 years. She wept openly
while we watched the hero die just before the rains returned.

Aunt Harri wiped her eyes, "I feel a fool bawling like
that. Makes one think my bladder's too close to my eyes. But
the West was like that in the Dirty Thirties. Alberta was not
as bad as Saskatchewan." Aunt Harri quietly rocked for a
moment.

"Were you on the farm right through the thirties?" I
asked.

"No. Fred retired and we went to England in '32. Came
back in '36. It was still bad in the late '30s: dust, poor crops,
low price for grain. But we always had a few cattle and
chickens and hauled water to the garden, so we ate well. Not
nearly so bad off as those poor blighters in Saskatchewan."

"You were lucky to live in Alberta," I ventured.

"No not lucky. When Fred came to Canada with his
family and first wife, he intended to go to Saskatchewan with

friends. He looked it over and kept on moving. He saw the danger of drought. In Alberta he homesteaded in parkland—part prairie, part bush. The land rolled slightly and he had a coulee with water and grazing land. Very few of our neighbours left during the thirties. Still it was tough, really tough. Yes, and one or two good friends died before the good times returned. But their kids and grandkids still live there."

"What gave people the strength to hang on no matter what?" Anna asked.

"The people were tough. They had come with nothing from England, Scotland, Germany, Ukraine, Norway—places where they would never have owned a garden plot, let alone a farm. They were self-sufficient, tough, independent people. Maybe some did whine to the government, but I never met any. They accepted tough times as just another challenge to beat. They worked together and looked after each other."

"Didn't the government help with welfare payments?" I interrupted.

"They sent out some food: fish and cheese as I remember. But some refused it. They felt able to look after themselves. The kind of people that settled the prairie accepted help only when they saw their children dying." Aunt Harri quit speaking and began waving her forefinger at me. She continued to do that for a full minute, her forehead wrinkled in thought.

"I hear the news," Aunt Harri finally spoke. "About all the people on welfare today. Often the children following in the parents' footsteps. Can you imagine what Canada would be like today if all the farmers on the prairies in the '30s had gone on welfare, the kind of welfare people expect today?"

Aunt Harri paused for me to answer, but I have learned caution. She went on: "Their grandchildren, three million people, would still be on welfare. The prairies would be a wasteland and Canada would be broke!"

ℒove has a ℒong Memory

Most people Aunt Harri's age appear tough and self-reliant; war and depression have groomed them, imparting the skills that equip them to contend with advancing years. I learned one day that Harriet Brown had trained on another battlefield: one of physical fear and emotional turmoil.

In a quiet corner of the lobby at Village Mews, I quite innocently asked her, "You once told me that Fred became ill six years after your wedding. What problem did he have?"

Aunt Harri's fingers tightened on her cane, her knuckles turned white, her face tensed, and her eyes squeezed shut. An emotional dam breached and tears ran down her cheeks.

"Dear God, what have I done," I thought, but said nothing aloud.

Aunt Harri pulled a huge man-size, linen handkerchief from the vee of her dress and wiped her eyes. I sucked in my breath when I saw the letter "F" embroidered on a corner. Fred died decades ago.

Aunt Harri poured out her story in a firm voice, occasionally wiping her eyes: "Fred was in his late fifties; I was 35. He had a grown family by his first wife, and then his second wife died. A year after our marriage, we retired to England, but the depression was hard so we returned to the farm in Alberta and started over.

"In 1938, soon after our daughter was born, Fred began losing touch. He'd stare into a corner and talk about things long gone. He'd have fits of temper, then, just as quickly, return to normal. The condition slowly worsened. His trips into the past got longer and the temper outbursts turned to rage. I began to live in terror. The local doctor finally signed him into the mental hospital in Ponoka, Alberta. They said he had hardening of the arteries of the brain.

"In the hospital he'd get better and they'd send him home, telling me to make sure he didn't worry. He'd stay well for a few months, then go off again. He went in and out four or five times before they kept him for good. I was his wife. I wanted him home and would keep him home until he got out of control.

"One time I heard him calling from his room. He was cringing in fear and staring at the animals on the ceiling. His animals were water stains on the plaster. Another time as he stood trimming his mustache with a pair of scissors, he suddenly turned on our oldest son with the scissors raised. I wrestled the scissors from him.

"Once he turned on me in a rage at the top of the stairs. I fought him with my back to the stairs; our middle child watched in terror from below. Fred had the strength of three men, but with God's help I got him back to his room.

"Paul, an alcoholic neighbour, often helped me. He could handle Fred when no one else could. He humoured him. For one whole day Fred's damaged mind took him back to the Boer war. Fred wrote military dispatches and Paul delivered them. I guess Paul's own problem helped him understand Fred.

"Whenever Fred was home and starting to go off, I kept a lamp burning in an upper window. The neighbours knew that if the lamp went out they must come quickly. I lived in fear and terror, but I wouldn't let them take my Fred back to the hospital until I could no longer handle him. I loved him.

"Eventually my own health broke, and I moved to Ontario with the kids. That was just as difficult as staying. I felt I had left him, deserted him."

Aunt Harri wiped her eyes with the handkerchief, then fingered the monogram. "Hard to find real linen handkerchiefs today. I always keep one on me—so I don't forget Fred."

An Encounter with Joy

Anna said, "I want to buy a bag of toffees for Aunt Harri," then in a moment, she disappeared. Never shop with a woman! She had corkscrewed down the aisle tossing goodies into the cart, and then sped around a mountain of tinned tuna. I waited, dreaming about the good things she would buy.

I didn't wait long, for a chill blast brought me to my senses. Anna's icy glare had reached me from the far end of the aisle. She held a box of pancake mix in her left hand and a shopping list in the other. She gestured in annoyance; I had the grocery cart!

I took off like a shot with the cart wheels castoring every which way. At that precise moment a slightly plump woman in a blue coat swung her cart at right angles—right in front of me. My grocery-laden lorry caught hers squarely abeam, knocking it over. The contents spilled onto the floor; a candy bag broke spewing toffees to the four winds. Blue Coat tumbled forward, but caught herself on the capsized cart just inches short of serious injury.

She muttered under her breath, but quickly brought herself and cart upright. I stood staring with my mouth wide open; Anna turned away in embarrassment as the store manager approached with a determined stride. Blue Coat shot me an icy look that easily outfrosted Anna's best glare. I read her mind, "Clumsy old coot!"

My own silent response showed little grace: "Woman driver!"

I eventually got my mouth shut, regained my composure, and muttered, "I'm sorry. I started up rather quickly. I do hope you're not hurt."

"I'm okay. Nothing damaged but my pride," she said icily, watching me with suspicion.

The manager listened to our exchange, and said, "I am glad no one got hurt. Don't worry about the candies ma'am, just get another bag. I'll sweep up the spilled ones."

My protagonist diffused the tension somewhat with, "Just a visitor here. Popped in to get some toffees for my mother—her favourite candy. She lives nearby."

We nodded and separated, Blue Coat carefully avoiding the business end of my cart. I thought, "I should know that woman, but I can't place her. Maybe she just reminds me of someone, even clips her sentences in a familiar way." I shrugged and hurried after Anna.

We saw Blue Coat leave the store and drive briskly away—without cutting anyone off. As though reading my thoughts, Anna said, "She certainly looked familiar, but I don't know why."

After taking our groceries home, we headed for Village Mews to deliver the toffees to Aunt Harri. I remembered with chagrin the other toffees on the supermarket floor.

Aunt Harri's door stood partially open. We could see the oldster in her recliner struggling to open a bag of toffees—can't we get away from those things? Calling out, "Hello Aunt Harri," I cavalierly threw the door open for Anna. A lady, until then hidden from our view, but now propelled by the fast-moving door, staggered forward on one foot and landed across the bed. A half-removed snow boot broke free and landed in Aunt Harri's lap.

"You again!" roared the woman from the supermarket.

I thought, "Now I am in trouble."

Canting her head on one side, she screwed up her eyes and frowned. "Thought you looked familiar," she said, sticking out her hand. "You're the character who writes about Mother. I'm Harriet Brown's daughter, Joy Forest."

As we shook hands, tension dissolved into laughter.

Aunt Harri spoke: "Nice if one of you rowdies'd collect this boot and get my toffees off the floor."

Aunt Harri Plans a Trip

As we entered Aunt Harri's room one winter day, she looked up from a pile of travel folders and announced, "I am going to England; I am going home."

"You're moving back to England?" I blurted in disbelief.

"No, no. Planning a trip to England—just a visit. Figure I should go before I lose the rest of my sight. I'll go in the spring with the flowers in bloom, say in April. Spring is much earlier in England."

"Do you really think . . .," I stammered. "I mean will your health—your strength—take it."

"Are you asking if the trip might kill me, if I might die on the way?" responded Aunt Harri bluntly. "So what if I do? England is just as close to heaven as is Canada."

At that, I gulped, and dropped into a chair. I noticed a grin play across Anna's mouth and a twinkle dance in her eye. Dumbly, I wondered, "Am I missing something?"

"Here's what I figure," proclaimed Aunt Harri as she spread out a map of Britain. "I will land at Heathrow and get a taxi to Ealing Common. Margaret still lives there. We can take the tube up to Victoria Station for day trips. Spend a week or two there before moving on. Don't want Margaret to overdo it; she must be close to 75. Then it's off to King's Lynn and Norwich. Not sure how I'll get there."

Anna jumped in with, "You could get one of those BritRail passes. You can travel all over England with one of those—even go up to Scotland."

I never said a word, but I thought plenty: "Anna don't encourage her. The old girl is worried about wearing out her 75-year-old friend, but she's pushing 100 herself."

Anna and Aunt Harri leaned over the map as Anna traced

her finger northward to Scotland. "If you get to Edinburgh," she said, be sure to visit the castle. We didn't see much of it because they had a military thing going on that day. We really enjoyed the Camera Obscura right next door."

I gently kicked Anna's foot to catch her eye and fired off a disapproving look. I got no response, but did catch a knowing expression passing between Anna and Aunt Harri.

Aunt Harri nodded her head vigorously and said, "That's a lot of train travel for an old biddy like me. I really should have someone take me around with a car."

The two women remained silent for a moment. I imagined brain waves passing between them—scheming, manipulating, telepathic signals. They turned to me like two heads on one neck, but only Aunt Harri's mouth moved: "You two could come with me —at least for part of the time. We could rent an Austin or something and drive up to Norfolk and Scotland."

I just gulped as Anna slowly nodded her head. Aunt Harri took our body language as acceptance and plowed right on, "If we go that far, we might as well drive up through the Highlands to Inverness and come down Loch Ness."

At that moment the dinner gong sounded. As we got up to leave I thought, "Saved by the bell."

Outside, I turned to Anna and sputtered: "Why did you encourage her? She couldn't possibly survive a trip like that. You know how stubborn she is; we'll never talk her out of it."

Anna gave me an 'oh, men' look and said, "She knows much better than you that she can't take it. You've been had. She has no intention of actually going; she'll just plan it. Half the fun of any trip comes from the planning, so don't deny her that."

I felt a mixture of embarrassment and relief as we drove away, until Anna said, "Stop at that travel agent for some brochures on Scotland."

Christmas Brings Pleasure—and Guilt!

When we discovered Aunt Harri had stayed at Village Mews throughout the holidays, it caused us some dismay. We thought it strange, even cruel, that her daughter Joy, or one of her sons, had not invited her to spend time with them. It seems that every time I pick up a paper I read something about elder abuse. Surely leaving an oldster all alone during the Christmas and New Year's celebrations must constitute one of the worst forms of elder abuse.

I stewed about this for a few busy weeks before blocking out an afternoon to call on her. When I realized how many weeks had lapsed since our last visit, I felt a pang of guilt. I consoled myself by saying, "She isn't my relative. She's just a friend, a former neighbour."

We found her in her recliner listening to a talking book, a John Grisham thriller. She stopped it immediately and seated us in her only other chairs: a tiny rocker and an equally small chair that might have belonged with a sewing machine. We chatted for a few minutes, while wondering how to raise the question of supposed abuse.

A sharp rap sounded at the door. We turned to see a nurse entering, carrying a small tray. She smiled brightly at all of us, then spoke to Aunt Harri, "Mrs. Brown, I have your new patch."

"Oh, good," replied Aunt Harri as she began rolling up her left sleeve. "Put it on this side. I can take the last one off the other arm myself."

We watched in puzzlement as the nurse laid out two

strips of clear tape. She then placed what looked like a cigarette paper across the tape. The ends of the tape protruded beyond the paper. Next, she squeezed a white paste from a tube onto the paper. As Aunt Harri finished rolling up her sleeve, the nurse stuck the whole mess onto her arm. The nurse gathered her things and waved goodbye. We waited while Aunt Harri rolled down her left sleeve, rolled up the other, and removed an identical patch from her right arm.

When Aunt Harri had completed this amazing performance, she said, "There we go. All done for another few hours."

"Exactly what is that?" I enquired.

"Nitroglycerin," Aunt Harri answered. "Heart medicine. Each patch lasts 12 hours. Absorbs through the skin instead of taking pills."

"Oh," I said, not knowing what else to say. I thought, "Good heavens, she has to put up with this, and at the same time suffer from elder abuse. Remembering why we came, I said, "Did you have a good Christmas? I don't think we have seen you since then."

"Had a quiet Christmas. Kids wanted me to come to the family do, but my heart couldn't take the strain of all those great-grandkids. My daughter and one son came to visit, and my other son called from out west."

"Don't you find it difficult staying alone?" Anna asked.

Aunt Harri pursed her lips, looked upwards, and sat quietly for a full minute before answering, "The Lord has allowed me to get this way, but with it He has given me contentment to accept things the way they are. I no longer have a desire to go places."

When we rose to leave, Aunt Harri said, "Been over six weeks since your last visit. Try to get back sooner next time."

I left thinking about nitro patches, heart problems, and a special dispensation of patience, and said to Anna: "Six weeks? Maybe we have been guilty of elder abuse."

Aunt Harri
Lands her Best Punch

"You do have to learn to take care of yourself and sometimes other people," said Aunt Harri one winter day as we sat visiting in Village Mews. We had arrived at the seniors' home about a half hour earlier and found Aunt Harri in a pensive mood. The doctor had recently ordered her to a wheelchair due to a heart flutter. She sat in it without saying a word.

To keep the conversation going, I ventured, "I guess you had to defend yourself a few times during the war."

Aunt Harri just nodded. She seemed intent on examining her white cane, running her fingers around a dent in the white plastic near the foot. After another minute she sighed, placed the cane across her knee, smiled, and said, "Yes, when you have been in the war, and cared for three children by yourself, you do remember some bad moments."

The oldster paused for a few seconds then continued, "Once during the first war, in France, a labourer on the pier grabbed me by the shirt-front and started speaking to me in a foreign language. I gave him a one-two in the ribs. He let go and ran off yelling in English, 'No goodie! no goodie!' I also recall a couple of soldiers who got fresh. Both of them found this little WAAC carried quite a punch. Years later a man arrived at the farmhouse when Fred was away. Said he was looking for work . . ."

Before Harriet could finish the sentence, she turned to a passing nurse, squinted with her head turned to one side and said, "That you Bertha?"

"Yes Aunt Harri."

"How is Old Downey?" asked Aunt Harri.

"Just some bruises. The hospital found no broken bones. He should come home tomorrow."

Aunt Harri dismissed the nurse with a nod and a wave of the hand. As the nurse moved out of earshot, Aunt Harri blurted, "Silly old fool!"

"Who, the nurse?" I asked.

"No, Old Downy. Acts like a teenager, a rude teenager, instead of an 86-year-old adult. Been getting worse lately. Often says suggestive things to the nurses. Recently, he's been scooting up behind them in his wheelchair, and slapping their backsides. Someone should have stopped him long ago."

"Did someone finally stop him?" Anna asked.

Aunt Harri hesitated just perceptibly before answering, "I was in my chair, coming out of the dining hall. Saw Bertha and stopped for her to pass. Old Downey came wheeling along behind her and raised his hand to whack. Just then something went wrong with his wheelchair. It spun sideways, bounced off mine, and dumped the old coot on the floor. Sure caused a ruckus. Didn't hurt me. Could have killed him."

Aunt Harri's mood seemed much brighter as we rose to leave. Near the door we met a maintenance man examining a wheelchair while the superintendent watched. Within our hearing, the man spoke to the super, "This is the chair that threw Downey. I can't find anything wrong with it, except for slight dents in the frame and one spoke. It's almost as though someone stuck a stick through the wheel."

I looked over his shoulder at the dents, walked slowly back to Aunt Harri, and sat beside her. Without saying a word, I reached over and ran my fingers across the similar dents in her cane.

Aunt Harri spoke, "Couldn't possibly have been me. I'm nearly blind. Anyway, I aimed for the old fool's arm."

"Aunt Harri," I said, "I won't tell a soul, but I really think someone should give you a medal."

Into The Teeth of the Storm

"This must be the dumbest thing we have ever done!" Anna grumbled as we peered through a frosted windshield into the worst snowstorm of the season.

"No," I answered, "When it comes to dumb, we should get a listing in the Guiness Book of Records. Remember when we drove on the Trans-Canada across Manitoba and Saskatchewan during a blizzard. We had to crash the car through deep snow drifts because the highways department had pulled off the snowplows."

Anna continued, "Or when we came home from Africa in the winter and borrowed my mother's car. Snow kept blowing into the engine and stalling it. It usually stopped as we pulled into a busy highway."

"We did promise Aunt Harri we'd come today and read some columns to her friends at Village Mews," I said, just as the car fishtailed on a patch of bare ice, hit a snowbank, and skidded into the ditch.

"We'll be here for hours," Anna muttered. "We should have stayed on the highway. If there's a farmhouse near, we'll never find it in this storm."

She had barely got out the words when a pickup truck coming from the other direction stopped. Three young men jumped out and surrounded our little car. Anna slid behind the wheel and I got out into the storm. With four of us pushing and Anna driving we easily got the car back onto the road.

"Icy patch," I said to the young men.

"Gotta watch that stuff Old Timer," said one of them.

"Old Timer!" I thought. That annoyed me so much, I almost forgot to call, "Thank you," through the storm.

I got back behind the wheel and readjusted the rear-view mirror. That's how I happened to see the truck accelerate away, strike the icy patch, do a 180, and back into the ditch. I put the car into reverse and started back toward them.

"Where are you going?" demanded Anna.

"Look behind. We just traded places with our guardian angels," I said.

To make a long story short, I attached our tow line to pull, Anna drove, they and I pushed, I grumbled, they cursed, and Anna yelled encouragement and direction. We fell on our faces in the snow, bruised our shoulders, froze our fingers and toes, and finally got the thing out. Exhausted and upset we continued to Village Mews.

"You're late!" said Aunt Harri from her wheelchair. "The folks are waiting for you down in the common room."

As we started down the hallway with me pushing and Anna walking beside the chair, Aunt Harri talked incessantly, thrilled with the chance to introduce her 'writer friends' to the gathered group of seniors. "Looks like a bad day. But I remember some real lulus on the prairies. Used to travel in cutters in the winter. One evening, going across the fields to a meeting with neighbours, we got lost. Wandered around their back field for an hour before his wife got out and led the way with a lantern. Many's the time the cutter tipped over and dumped us all. Even going to the well for water during a blizzard was an adventure. Time you got to the house the wind had blown away half the water—most of it got frozen to your clothes so you could hardly walk. Frostbite was more common then than winter sniffles today."

Aunt Harri quit chattering as we entered the common room, but picked up the theme as she introduced us: "I was just saying how easy winter travel is today. Folks just get into a nice warm car and drive on a plowed highway regardless of the weather. Never have the adventures we old-timers had —and we usually got to places on time."

A Prairie Journey

Aunt Harri had loaned me a box of old pictures, newspaper clippings and other memorabilia. I had taken them home, put them in a drawer, and forgotten all about them.

A week later I couldn't sleep, so I made a cup of tea and moved to my recliner. Remembering Aunt Harri's box of memories, I got them out of the drawer and began perusing the contents.

I saw pictures of people in army uniforms, on board a ship, gathered outside a church, at the door of a farm house, and posed before old cars. I recognized Aunt Harri in many and identified the distinguished man with the mustache as Fred. I began to get sleepy.

Then I found a shot of an old car with Harriet and Fred standing at the driver's door—an Overland, I guessed. Packed for a journey, it had a trunk strapped on the rear, a jerry can on the running board, and canvas side curtains in place. I wondered where they were going as I shut my eyes, snuggled back in my chair, and found myself in another world.

"Comfortable back seat in this car," I called out to Fred at the wheel."

Fred nodded as he guided the big machine along a dirt prairie road at a steady 35. Dust devils leaped from our wheels as we raced past sloughs, fields of grain, and clap-board farm buildings. Fred carefully kept to the smoothly-packed tracks between the deep wagon ruts.

"Keep it rolling Fred, we want to get there tonight," encouraged Aunt Harri.

"We'll make Edmonton in four hours if we can keep this up," answered Fred.

But we didn't. Pleasant summer clouds quickly turned ugly, dumping their contents and turning the road to grease. Fred shifted down and fought the wheel to keep out of the ditch. We had slowed to 15. Day turned to night and the rain continued; soon the wheels became clogged with mud. Fred dropped into first gear and pushed the big car on, swerving and sliding, and plowing deep ruts into the road-become-quagmire.

"We can't go on like this," Fred called above the labouring engine. "I'll find a place to pull off."

"Bang-shhhhh," answered the right rear tire.

"That really caps it," muttered Aunt Harri.

Fred and I got out; the rain soaking through my clothes like warm tea. We removed the flat, putting the wheel nuts on the running board. The rain stopped and Aunt Harri got out to stretch, accidentally kicking the nuts into the darkness and mud. Fred and I mounted the spare by borrowing nuts from the other wheels.

As we climbed into the car, Aunt Harri said, "We'll sleep right here. Only idiots would come out on a night like this."

At about six in the morning I aroused to a glow in the eastern sky. We all stretched and looked into the still-overcast gloom. "That's not the sun coming up!" Aunt Harri said in sudden terror.

The glow turned into a powerful headlight and rushed toward us; the blast of a steam whistle shook the car. Seconds later an engine pulling ten coaches passed yards in front of us, sending the car rocking on its springs. I grabbed for the arm rests as my seat continued to rock back and forth. Then someone rested a hand on my shoulder.

"Wake up! You slept all night in your chair. And you spilled your tea down your PJs!" Anna called as she continued rocking my chair. "Move it—we promised to take Aunt Harri for a drive in the country today."

I stumbled toward the bathroom muttering about touring

cars, prairie downpours, muddy roads, and unmarked crossings. Anna called after me, "Have you cracked up?"

"Not quite," I answered. "The train missed us by five yards."

Aunt Harri takes Charge

One beautiful spring day, we found Aunt Harri sitting in her wheelchair at the front entrance of Village Mews seniors' home. She had a clipboard in her left hand and a coloured marker in her right. She didn't see us approaching—partly due to her poor eyesight, and partly because she had fixed her attention on the far end of the circular drive. I looked over her shoulder to see the names of about ten people written in one-inch letters on a sheet of note paper on the clipboard. I also noticed a small brass bell in her lap—the kind school teachers once used to call the kids in from recess.

"What are you up to?" I asked.

Aunt Harri jumped: "You startled me! I'm waiting for the bus."

"This is not a bus stop," I ventured.

"'Tis today. Should be here now. I arranged for some of our folks to join a garden tour. He's late. Don't know why some men can't keep time. He's likely gabbing with another driver somewhere—and they accuse women of gossiping."

Even as she spoke a large coach pulled in and stopped with its door opposite Aunt Harri. Through the windows I could see passengers half filling the bus. Out of the corner of my eye I noticed Aunt Harri's features harden, and suspected she planned to tear a strip off the driver for tardiness. The door swung open and the driver stepped down—a young woman, looking sharp in a blue uniform. "Sorry I'm late," she said. "Are the folks ready; they weren't at the last place."

Rarely have I seen Aunt Harri at a loss for words. She just gulped, turned her chair and shot back to the building. Pulling the door ajar, she rang the bell loud and long. Almost immediately a man in white stepped through and held the door open. As the folk started out, Aunt Harri positioned herself next to the driver at the bus door. As the first lady approached, leaning heavily on a cane, Aunt Harri strained forward, said, "Betty," put a check beside the name, then as the driver helped Betty aboard, she called after her, "Don't lose your cane this time."

Next came Mr. Nolan. As Aunt Harri checked him off, she said, "Nolan, do keep your teeth in your mouth." Nolan called back something rude as he disappeared into the coach.

A lady in a wheelchair came next. She parked it at the luggage compartment and walked unsteadily on the driver's arm toward the bus door. Aunt Harri's, "Whoa," brought them to a halt.

"That chair isn't marked. Might get mixed up with someone else's," said Aunt Harri. With that she wheeled over to it, fished a piece of chalk from a pocket and marked the words "Anne—Village Mews" across the plastic seat back. She next marked the name Anne on her list and nodded for Anne and the driver to continue.

As I watched Aunt Harri continuing her task, I couldn't help but notice all of the Village Mews passengers were at least ten years younger than the bossy oldster. When the tenth disappeared into the bus, she waved and called, "All accounted for; good trip."

Only when the coach disappeared from view, did Aunt Harri turn to us. "You're not going?" I questioned.

"Not this time," she answered. "I just arrange the trips and make sure everyone gets safely on board—and off when they return. You just wouldn't believe how helpless these old people can be if someone doesn't look after them."

Bert Takes Control

Bert Smells Smoke

When Bert called one Saturday afternoon, asking if I could meet him for coffee, I rubbed my hands with glee. Every time this guy shows up, something memorable happens. Bert is my great half uncle, or second cousin twice removed, or something or other. In our mixed-up family, due to our patriarch's two marriages separated by 40 years, no one knows for sure who is what. Bert carries over 200 pounds on his big-boned, 63-year-old frame. Only his mother ever used his real name: Egbert.

Bert made it to Grade 10 before discovering the teachers knew less than he did about most subjects. When he tried to educate them they reacted negatively, so he didn't return the following year. In ten years he became the resident expert in his home town. His personal book collection outgrew the town library in both numbers and quality.

Often some local wit would think he had bested Bert during a round-table discussion, only to hear him say, "I have a book on that subject." He would rush home, return with a well-worn volume, and drive the point home until the debater conceded or collapsed in confusion. Everyone either hates or loves Bert; no one ignores him.

Bert beat me to the donut shop by a minute. He wheeled his old K-car up beside an identical model and began studying the other car in detail. When I approached, I found him looking from the interior of one to the other, as though evaluating or comparing. "Want it for spare parts?" I asked.

He just grunted and headed for the shop. We ordered and

began to chat about old times, but, across the room, a narrow-chested, middle-aged man with a whining voice caught our attention. The smoke from Narrow Chest's cigarette drifted across to us in the non-smoking section. We started to eavesdrop.

"They're fanatics. Nothing but fanatics," Narrow Chest declaimed as he parried and thrust his cigarette to emphasize his point. "They want to impose their will on the rest of us, about one third of the population. The anti-smoking fanatics have no concern about the problems they have brought on society by forcing their agenda on the rest of us."

I heard Bert wheeze asthmatically as Narrow Chest took a couple of puffs and checked his immediate audience for reaction. Getting none, he continued, "I don't believe the scaremongers, but if I do injure my health, that's my business not theirs."

At that point he got a reaction from an unexpected source. "Bull, bull, and double bull," thundered Bert as he heaved his bulk across the room and stopped with one hand on Narrow Chest's table, eyeballing him one on one (actually, Bert added another syllable to the word 'bull').

"You sir are the fanatic, the addict, the user who wants to force his agenda on society. Just come outside for a moment and I will show you the evidence," roared Bert.

Narrow Chest and his friends thought Bert was spoiling for a fight, so I said, "Do you have a book on smoking in your car?"

"Not a book," he answered, "some other evidence."

Narrow Chest and friends agreed to follow Bert outside, who positioned himself between the two cars. "This is your car," Bert said, tapping the roof of the second K-car.

Narrow Chest looked puzzled, but nodded.

Bert continued, "Look at the fabric on the interior, especially on the roof. See how yellow it is compared to my car. Both cars are the same age. Crap from cigarettes has coated the ceiling in yours. If your car's interior looks like that, imagine what your lungs look like. But we don't care about your lungs do we. Think about your wife's lungs, your kids' lungs and your friends' lungs."

Narrow Chest leaned down and looked into the car before turning to Bert with a puzzled look, "How did you know this was my car?"

Bert smirked, "By the smell, Buddy. By the smell."

Bert Goes back to School

Will Rogers said, "The schools ain't what they used to be and never was."

Bert picked me up for a ride in the country. He wouldn't tell me where he wanted to go on that blustery winter day. We travelled about 10 km on those straight, well-paved secondary roads that criss-cross southwestern Ontario, before entering a tree-lined avenue that wound along a riverbank. We slowed down as Bert studied the terrain.

"Here we are," said Bert as he swung the car into a yard and pulled up in front of a vacant, one-room schoolhouse. "It's for sale. I might buy it."

I looked carefully at the building, then back to Bert before saying, "It has much in common with you."

"Meaning what?" demanded Bert.

"Well," I answered, "It's old, looks a little shabby, seems creaky and decrepit, and certainly could use a face lift. It also sags in the middle."

"Not nice. I could use it for a workshop—a hideaway where I could work on crafts and hobbies."

I shook my head: "You old high-school dropout, you just

want the place so you can tell people you spent a lot more time in school."

After a long reflective pause, Bert said, "Does carry you back, doesn't it. Remember how we went to school as kids? Remember the school vans—especially in winter?"

Who could forget them? We began to reminisce. In central Alberta kids went to school in horse-drawn vans right up until 1950. The van left from near Bert's place and travelled for half an hour before getting to my place at about 6:30 in the morning. Two hours later we got to school. I arrived home that evening after 6:00—if all went well. In winter the vans rode on sleighs; you could hear sleigh bells and children singing for miles across the prairie.

Sometimes the van rolled over in deep snow drifts. The boys and girls would pile out and help the driver to set the van back on the sleigh. If they couldn't get the thing upright, they would take refuge in a farmhouse. The farmer's wife would administer first aid to eight or ten sets of frostbitten ears and noses—and sometimes fingers or toes.

Bert sighed, "Gosh, today city parents won't let their kids walk to school when the route crosses a busy road. And the country school buses don't even run on a snowy day. If a kid today had to help push a bus, the parents would sue the school board."

We settled back in the warmth of the car, looked at the old building, and went on reflecting. Bert reminded me about Miss Bell who used to strap me two or three times a week because I couldn't copy things correctly from the blackboard. I suffered for a year before a new teacher took a different approach. I spent the rest of primary school battling with arithmetic, wondering why I had so much trouble. Actually, I never learned about learning disabilities for another 40 years.

I reminded Bert about his school-yard battles. The bigger kids used to tease him because his father had spent time in a psychiatric hospital. Before the principle clued in, Bert took, and handed out, a few poundings. In Grade 10 Bert dropped out because the teachers knew less than he in most areas.

Bert commented: "Today, most teachers know about learning disabilities and discrimination. Kids can even use calculators. Teachers also have a much better education than they did when we went to school. No doubt about it; kids have it much easier today."

"Bert," I said, "If you had gone to school today, you might have finished high school, even gone to university."

Bert looked at me with a stunned look: "Are you kidding? If I had to go to school today it would bore me out of my skull. I'd drop out in Grade 2!"

Bert Enters the Brawl

Bert's call came just when I needed some distraction. Following a few moments of chat, I agreed to join him at a community meeting on television violence. "It's a lady speaking," he said. "She heads an association against TV violence. I thought it might give you an idea for a column."

Before he hung up, I said, "I didn't know you watched television."

"I do, sometimes. Last year I logged 15 hours—total. As an adult, I couldn't find much else worth watching, but most children view twice that amount in a week—most of it violent garbage."

I hung up, but kept thinking about Bert. In his teens, doctors told him he had a serious heart condition. He never married because he didn't want to saddle a woman with a man who might drop dead at any moment. He likes children, caring much for those of friends and relatives.

I drove up country to Bert's village, picked him up, and

parked near the community hall. We entered just as the meeting started. The moderator introduced the speaker, a Mrs. 'Smith,' and explained that she would speak for 15 minutes, before opening the meeting for discussion.

Mrs. Smith spoke well, quoting from psychological surveys, reviewing the status of programs such as Power Rangers, and relating various CRTC and broadcaster decisions. When she graphically described some of the violence portrayed for the consumption of children, I felt a knot of anger tighten in my stomach. She went on to say, "I never personally watch television programs containing violence. I get too much reviewing programming for my job."

Smith also explained that she did not allow her children to watch violent TV shows, but noted that violence influenced them through playmates who did not face similar restrictions. She completed her speech to a burst of applause, and turned the session back to the moderator for discussion. He asked that participants step up to the audience microphone.

Three people in turn stood at their chairs and briefly thanked the speaker for her presentation. The fourth stepped confidently to the microphone. He looked about 22—I guessed a university student. When he began, he spoke articulately, displaying all the mental gymnastics of one skilled in debate.

His opening salvo caught most of us off guard. I can't remember everything he said, but he swayed us with his skill and style. He attacked the speaker's position without attacking her. In essence he said, "You propose a form of censorship. Society cannot tolerate even the thin edge of the wedge of censorship. You are imposing your standards on others. We must allow everybody to watch whatever they choose. If you don't like a TV show, turn it off. Do you believe in censorship?"

The speaker answered with a question, "Do you have children?"

"No, but that's irrelevant," returned the debater.

For the next ten minutes, the debate swayed back and forth. The speaker and debater matched thrust for thrust, both showing equal skill and courtesy. The audience sat spellbound. The debater had only one theme, "Any attempt to control TV violence amounts to censorship, which is always wrong."

I saw Bert preparing to stand and grabbed at his sleeve, but not quickly enough. He leaped to his feet and bellowed loudly, "Red herring! Red Herring!"

The speaker and debater stopped talking and turned to Bert.

"Red herring," Bert repeated. "Censorship has nothing to do with the issue. Mrs. Smith has appealed to a primal right that predates modern notions of human rights. She demands the right as a mother to protect her children from danger from all sources. You appeal to freedom of speech for selfish purposes. You have yet to learn that no man can face an angry mother protecting her children."

The hall erupted in applause. The debater turned red and sat down. Bert grinned at me and said, "The heck with the niceties of debate. This issue really calls for a school-yard brawl."

Bert Wades in

"The world is filled with verbal do-gooders," said Bert as we sat in front of his wood stove one Saturday evening.

"Verbal do gooders?" I reacted.

"Yes, verbal do-gooders. People who call in to radio talk shows to sound off about some little thing that offended an element of society. Feminists who rant and rave in the media about the violence of men. Animal-rights activists who put animals ahead of humanity. Environmentalists who howl about the destruction of our earth. Anti-gun people who would disarm hunters."

Bert paused long enough to toss me a knowing look. Although we agree on many things, we differ on others. Bert hunts avidly; I have problems with needless killing of living things. I might accept hunting if deer and geese could shoot back. Although I admit that idea clashes with my stand against violence.

"Do you feel those 'verbal do-gooders' have no right to voice their opinions?" I asked.

Bert glared at me: "They have every right. I just wish more of them would turn their vocal output into action— positive action. They need to get involved in righting the wrongs instead of whining and hoping the government or someone else will fix the problems for them. As Bert spoke, he picked up an official-looking envelope and tapped it against his knee."

"What is that?" I asked.

"A summons to appear in court as a witness," he answered.

"In what kind of a case," I probed.

"A domestic violence case. A big ugly cuss who beat on his tiny wife."

"You saw it happen?" I asked, my interest peaking.

"I not only saw it, I stopped it."

"Tell me all about it," I pleaded.

Bert hesitated for a long moment, I supposed he wondered what business it was of mine. Then he began to talk. The story went something like this. He had gone to the supermarket in the town a few miles from his village. He had noticed a well-dressed man verbally abusing his wife. The guy had seemed unhappy with the amount and type of groceries she had put in the basket. Bert had noticed a bruise on the

woman's cheek and, concerned for her welfare, stayed near
them as they entered a check-out line. At one point the couple
exchanged harsh words in whispers. The man then struck the
woman with a sudden elbow jab—done is such a way that
most people would never notice.

Bert's line finished first. He carried his groceries to the
car and watched for the couple as he stalled for time,
carefully packing his purchases into the trunk. As luck would
have it, the couple came to a big car next to Bert. As the
woman bent to enter, the man struck her, knocking her inside.
Bert, age about 64, weight over 200 pounds, moved quickly.
He confronted the younger man, who immediately cowered
back against the car. Bert ordered a passer-by to call the cops.
The police arrived quickly and charged the man based on the
testimony of Bert and the woman. Only after the police left,
did Bert realize he was still holding a large bottle of tomato
juice by the neck.

Bert finished his story, then said, "If you care, don't just
say it on phone-in talk shows, in letters to the editor, or in
public meetings. If you want to do something real, committees
and commissions have value—but concern about human issues
entails more than just verbosity or even emotional
vulnerability—it means more when you back it up with
physical vulnerability."

"But, he might have killed you!" I said.

"That's just the point. I wouldn't have been the first good
samaritan to die—or the last. But now I can live with a clear
conscience, knowing I had the courage to match my
convictions with action."

Bert Decides to Vote with His Feet

Bert arrived uninvited just before lunch one Saturday. Bert calls on friends and receives visitors without thought of formalities such as invitations. That is just one of his special and endearing qualities. Without comment I put another plate on the table and looked in the refrigerator for a wider assortment of sandwich makings. With Anna away visiting grandchildren, I go for the simplest of meals.

We sat eating without speaking, simply enjoying the contentment that comes with the presence of a lifelong friend. A sense of unease tugged at me when I realized we had been eating for five minutes, but Bert had made none of his usual friendly critiques of my eating style. He eats meat, I don't.

As though reading my thoughts, Bert said, "Don't choke on your tofu when I lay this on you, but I'm going back."

I nearly gagged on my veggie wiener. "Going back?" I responded in disbelief. "You've only been here for five years. What about your house? Your job? Your family and friends?"

Bert just shrugged and continued eating. You have to know Bert. He moved from Alberta to Ontario as a child at about the same time I did. I adopted Ontario, content to visit Alberta every few years, but Bert—who never married—retained a loyalty to his birthplace and moved back and forth over the years.

Bert finally spoke, "I'll keep the house as an investment. I have friends and family in both places. Richard has a part-time job lined up—that's all I need."

"But," I stammered, "what about the sub-zero winters, blistering hot summers, miles of open country, lack of forests, millions of mosquitoes, poor roads, and . . ."

"Just can it," interrupted Bert. "You still think of the place you knew as a kid. Alberta has great roads and forests and mountains . . ."

This time I cut in, "And terrible winters . . ."

"And fabulous chinook winds," returned Bert. "And besides Alberta is just as close to Arizona as Ontario is to Florida."

"What about the mosquitoes?" I asked.

"They disappeared with the buffalo," snapped Bert.

Men do have difficulty expressing their feelings toward each other. I took a few bites of food to stall for time, then choked out, "The truth is Bert, I'll miss you."

He stared at me blankly, then muttered, "Yeah." After a moment's hesitation, he said, "But you'll live. After all you took off and moved to South Africa without giving much thought about who'd miss you. Alberta's not that far away, phone calls don't cost much, and I'll get hooked up to E-mail. And it will give you a reason to come west more often."

"Why are you moving now?" I asked.

"Uncle Bob," he answered.

Puzzled, I queried, "Uncle Bob?"

"Yeah. Uncle Bob, better known as Bob Rae. Right now he's preparing for an election by spending money. When he loses, the next government will have to pick up the bills and raise taxes. I'm fed up with paying higher and higher taxes from my part-time salary and the meagre investments I have. I earn less money then many people on welfare, but Pink Bob expects me to happily support them."

I should have anticipated Bert's reply. He lives his life according to conscience and a set of clearly-defined principles and votes with his feet when necessary; nevertheless, I still argued, "But you will still pay taxes."

"True, but less taxes. Alberta has no PST and a fiscally responsible government. I could write letters, whine, join a tax revolt, or attend anti-tax rallies, but I'd rather just move to a place that has got its act together."

"At least, you plan to remain loyal to Canada, to stand by the country," I commented.

Bert nodded emphatically, "Yes, and with Alberta leading the way, the federal government may yet fix its problems and stand by us."

Bert Loads His Shotgun

I laid down the paper after reading about a murder committed by teenagers just as Bert pulled into the driveway in his new pick-up. He recently bought it in preparation for his move back to Alberta. He got out, but didn't come straight to the house. He stood staring at the driver's door. Curious, I stepped outside and saw ugly scratches in the paint.

"They gouged it," Bert explained, "and slashed two tires."

"Who did," I asked.

"Kids. Young teenagers. Hoodlums."

"How do you know? Did you see them?" I quizzed.

"No, but my neighbour did. He chased them away before they did more damage. The police haven't caught them yet," said Bert looking thoroughly sour.

"Teenage crime has become a major problem," I said as we sat down in the livingroom.

"Various officials keep saying crime hasn't got any worse," but those of us who have been around for a few decades know better.

"I remember kids getting into trouble fifty years ago," I ventured.

Bert smiled: "Yeah like the time the Johnston kids put the milk delivery wagon on the roof of the town hall. Or the halloween someone moved old man Bennet's outhouse back three feet so he fell in the hole. Next year he waited for them with a shot gun loaded with rock salt. The McIntyre boys had trouble sitting down for weeks."

"Or the time someone wiggled through the cottage window at the lake and stole some cookies," I said looking straight at Bert.

Bert grimaced, gave me a vile look, then said, "There is a big difference between high-jinks like the ones we remember and property damage, armed robbery, and murder."

"What brought on the underage crime wave," I asked.

"The answer is so simple, so basic, no one wants to believe it. Kids today don't know right from wrong. No one has taught them the difference. George Foreman tells of mugging someone as a teenager, then wondering why the police wanted him. He didn't know mugging was wrong! Today's Canadian kids are the same. In my day I attended Sunday school. There the teacher put the fear of God in me—dangled me over the pit of Hell if I even considered breaking the least of the ten commandments."

"Oh come off it," I snapped back. "You walked out of church at age 17 and never went back except for weddings and funerals."

"True, but the basic teaching stuck. The concepts of good and bad stay for a lifetime. Not as many kids go to Sunday school today. Few get worthwhile teaching on moral issues in regular school because educators and political leaders are afraid to offend minorities. Modern life has robbed the family of time spent in activities designed to develop character. And to cap it all off, the law prevents a victim from responding in a way that would teach the little jackasses a lesson."

"Is it really that simple," I asked.

"It is. Recently, I read about a new branch of psychology

that concentrates on narrative—story telling if you like—as a means of learning. They suggest that people use stories as much as logic to order their lives. I believe if kids spend hours watching television stories that glorify criminal acts and violence, they will respond to life with violence."

"So you think we have filtered out all the good and provided only bad influences," I summarized.

"No. Not altogether, or every kid would turn out rotten. Parents need to make sure they smother their kids in worthwhile, positive, learning experiences," said Bert getting to his feet. "Meanwhile, I've got to get to town and find some rock salt. I hear salt acts as a purifying agent."

Alberta Bound

Bert arrived at my door carrying a box.

"I'm off to Alberta. I forgot to get rid of these things. Maybe you can use them or give them to someone else."

He sat the box on a chair and opened the lid to reveal an odd collection of bits and pieces: a hunter's hand warmer, a wind-up alarm clock, a lamp with no shade, a large doll with flaxen hair, a collection of toy trucks, and a cap pistol.

Bert stared into the box, then removed the cap pistol, dropping it into his pocket. He said, "No use leaving that with you. With your attitude to guns, I figure you'd throw it out. Give the other toys to your grandkids. I kept them around for neighbour kids when they came visiting."

Picking up the doll, Bert said, "I know your Julie or Bethany will love this. And boys always love trucks."

"What if the boys want the doll and the girls want the trucks?" I asked.

Letting out a snort of derision Bert—who loves kids but

has none of his own—said, "Girls always like dolls, and boys always like trucks."

Seeing a good argument, I said, "Oh! Doesn't psychology teach us that we socialize children to like the things society judges as most appropriate? If we don't influence them, boys would pick dolls as often as girls would."

Wagging his head, Bert said "There you go with the old 'nurture versus nature' argument. Girls pick dolls because of nature—motherhood is part of a baby girl before birth. And boys come with a predisposition towards aggression whether we like it or not. It's in their psyche; it's encoded in their genes."

Bert may not have finished high school, but he reads everything. On this issue, I tended to agree with him, but I had a good argument going and pushed it a little further: "Are you trying to tell me you were born with a love of guns and hunting? That you never had an inkling to hold a doll, or play with girls?"

Bert answered, "That's exactly what I'm telling you—with the exception of the bit about girls. Liking girls comes later as the hormones develop, and that just strengthens my point. Nature programs us in all we do. Kids who grow up differently, who like the wrong things, have a built-in problem."

I pretended to change the subject: "Remember when you were ill as a teenager? You had aggravated your heart condition, and the doctor ordered you to bed for a month. Do you remember what you did for entertainment?"

"I read books, mostly."

"You don't remember what else you did? I do. You sat in the second-story bedroom window of your prairie home and shot gophers with your rifle. You aimed at the entrance to the burrow and waited until one popped up its head, then bang. The whole countryside talked about your marksmanship."

At that point, Anna brought us tea. She gave me an

encouraging look, indicating she was happy I had veered
away from the argument. We sat chatting, drinking tea, and
eating muffins for a half hour, before Bert rose to leave.

We said our goodbyes and Bert put his hand on the
doorknob to leave, but I stopped him with another question:
"Besides reading and shooting gophers, can you remember
what else you did?"

Bert nodded, "Yes mother taught me to knit. When I got
tired of reading and the weather kept the gophers underground, I spent my time knitting."

Realizing the implication of his admission, Bert reddened
and left. I called after him, "Nurture or nature?"

Anna snapped at me, "He had one point right. Men are
naturally aggressive, whether hunting or arguing. And when it
comes to friendship, they are born stupid."

The Mounties Get their Man

Less than a week after Bert's departure for Alberta, I received
a disturbing phone call.

It went something like this, "Mr. Wiseman?"

"Yes, speaking."

"Constable Weston here, RCMP, Pontex, Saskatchewan.
Do you have a friend named Egbert Stone?" the voice
queried.

"Yes," I answered as a knot formed in my stomach. I
could already see Bert dead on the highway. "What's wrong?
Is he all right?" I demanded.

"He's fine. Just a routine inquiry. How long have you
known Mr. Stone?"

"Nearly all his life. He's a relative and good friend. Is he
in some kind of trouble?"

"Nothing serious. He said you would vouch for him. Has he ever been in any kind of trouble with the opposite sex?"

"Never! He's an old-fashioned gentleman. More than once he has risked personal danger when he caught someone threatening a woman or child," I answered with conviction, but I wondered what goofy thing he had done this time.

"Oh . . ., you have helped very much. Thanks, and don't worry about Mr. Stone," the voice said before ringing off.

I worried for a week until Bert's letter arrived. I'll tell his story as he told it in the letter.

Bert had not hurried west, but visited along the way. A week after leaving he stopped at a village called Mortlach on the Trans Canada Highway in Saskatchewan. There he set up his camp stove and prepared an evening meal. He would drive for two or three more hours then stop for the night.

He looked up from his meal and saw her. The young woman wore a large backpack and towed a roller board—one of those small wheeled suitcases you carry onto airplanes. She left the village and headed west down the highway, the roller board's wheels bumping on the gravel shoulder. Bert had muttered something about the foolishness of young female hitchhikers looking for trouble, but put her out of his mind.

A half hour later as Bert prepared to leave, he noticed a red pickup cruising the village streets. Its young driver eyed each of the two or three young women on the streets. Bert drove out of town.

At the first crossroad he saw Miss Backpack and decided to offer her a ride. "Thanks," she said much too curtly, "I'm waiting for the bus."

Bert drove on, but through his rear-view mirror noticed the red pickup stop for the hitchhiker. He thought he saw an altercation; the young woman climbed into the cab. Concerned, Bert pulled onto the shoulder and let them pass. From a hundred metres behind he could see the young woman arguing with the driver. Bert dropped back and followed them. They turned south on Highway 19, west on a sideroad, then zigzagged up and down farm roads. When they reached a village the two got out and the driver hurried the young woman into a house. Both seemed agitated.

Not sure what to do next, Bert parked nearby and watched the house. Just as he wished for a cell phone to call the police, an officer tapped on his window.

It took an hour of explanations to straighten it out. Bert explained, he wasn't stalking the couple; he thought he had witnessed an abduction. The couple, who had called the police from the house, explained how she had marched off in a snit when he didn't meet her on time in Mortlach. When the couple saw Bert following, the same guy who had attempted to pick her up, they tried to shake him, then headed for a friend's home.

After the policeman called me, everyone laughed and apologized all around.

"I felt stupid," Bert said later by phone, "but not as bad as I would've felt had it been the real thing and I ignored it."

Living on the Hazy Edge of Consciousness

I sat bolt upright in the middle of the night, sweat running down my back. The night seemed quiet outside the window, yet something had wakened me. Assisted by streetlights, a full moon chased the darkness away save for areas where shrubs huddled close to buildings. As I listened and watched, one lone pick-up drove quietly along the street.

Maybe I had not adjusted to the move from the country, and some town noise had reached me. I stood looking out the window. Still nothing stirred until the lights of a car, no a pick-up truck, appeared. As it made its way slowly westward, it looked like the same vehicle. I could dimly see one large person at the wheel. "Looks familiar," I thought. "Like Bert's truck, but Bert's in Alberta."

Puzzled, I turned quietly back toward my bed to avoid waking Anna in the next room. A chill ran down my spine and perspiration beaded on my forehead. Had I been dreaming some foolish nightmare? Or maybe I had developed a fever. I wandered back to the window to see the same pick-up returning very slowly. It nearly stopped in front of the building, then moved on to hesitate momentarily once more before continuing out of sight. In the moonlight I could clearly see a plastic tool chest mounted in the box immediately behind the cab. "Bert has a box exactly like that," I said aloud.

I sat on the bed and began a mental debate: "Why would Bert have come back to Ontario? Because Bert does crazy things like that. Why is he driving up and down the street? Because he has never visited us at the apartment—he's not sure of our address." I dashed back to the window. Bert's truck crawled past again.

Immediately I scrambled into my clothes. Slipping quietly out of the house, I sat on the front steps watching for Bert's truck to return. Within five minutes, it reappeared, moving quietly, slowing even more as it neared the building. I stood up, waved, and walked toward the curb. Instead of stopping, the pick-up accelerated suddenly, slewing sideways and leaving tire marks on the street. I did not get a clear view of the driver.

Shaken, I said aloud to myself, "That couldn't have been Bert." As I turned back to the front door, two dark figures appeared between the buildings and ran down the street in the direction of the disappearing pick-up. Confused, and maybe not fully awake, I went inside and dropped into my chair.

As my fuzzy mind cleared and I fully grasped that Bert had not returned, I realized I had witnessed something mighty suspicious. Again, I spoke aloud to myself, "Call the police you dummy!" and reached for the telephone.

Before I could touch the thing it rang, making me snatch my hand back as though from fire. Half way through the second ring, I recovered and grabbed it, "Hello."

Bert's voice spoke clearly in my ear, "Ray, that you? Are you all right?"

"Of course I am fine. Bert, where are you calling from?"

"From my little house in Gawain, Alberta. Where else would I call from in the middle of the night."

"Bert," I asked, "surely you didn't call just to ask me how I am?"

"I did just that. I woke a few minutes ago with a feeling of foreboding. I'd been dreaming about you getting killed or injured in a house burglary. I couldn't get it out of my mind."

"Bert, thanks for calling. I'm fine; I'll write." We rang off.

Things like this do happen, some would say as divine intervention; others would argue for a human sixth sense. But aren't friends wonderful, there when you need them, even on the hazy edge of consciousness.

Bert Makes Legal Sense

Following the Supreme Court decision concerning tobacco advertising I read a little on the history and authority of the Court. Good thing I did, but maybe I didn't read enough.

"You Easterners have done it again!" Bert's voice thundered across 3,000 kilometres of telephone wire.

"Bert," I answered, "You have been back in Alberta for

only a few months, and already you sound like a rabid western nationalist. Now what have we done to offend you?"

"That dumb decision by the Supreme Court on tobacco advertising," he snorted.

"Bert, the Supreme Court belongs to all of Canada, not just the East. Judges get appointed from across the country."

"True. I guess," Bert conceded. "But Easterners just seem to dominate in everything that happens. There are just too many of you. Anyway where does that gaggle of senior citizens get the authority to overrule the parliament of Canada? I thought in a British-style parliamentary system, parliament was supreme."

"Trudeau," I answered.

"Trudeau?"

I explained, "Yes Trudeau did it. The Supreme Court has long had the responsibility to interpret constitutional issues, but Trudeau passed the Charter of Rights and Freedoms, consequently strengthening the Supreme Court's position. Now if the Court thinks the lawmakers erred by violating someone's rights, it rules the law unconstitutional based on the Charter. Parliament now finds it difficult to have the final say."

"Is that right or proper?" Bert asked.

"Whether it's right or not, that's what they do. Some people doubt the democracy of the system, and this case makes a good example. In parliament our elected officials passed an anti-smoking law that every party agreed to. Now nine appointed judges who answer to no one struck down the law."

Bert probed further, "That's interesting, but if they are appointed political hacks, what do they know about the law? Why should their opinion count?"

"I hope they're not just hacks. Before appointment, they must have served as judges or had at least ten years experience at the bar. As Supreme Court justices, they must give legal opinions based on law, not just personal bias."

"But that is just the problem," roared Bert. "They all had their own slant on it. They disagreed on the main issue, voting five one way and four the other. If they are the country's best legal brains and base their decisions on law, how come they couldn't come to a single conclusion."

I didn't know what to say; Bert continued anyway. "Let's take any one of those judges, and put him or her back in a courtroom. Let's imagine the judge trying an accused murderer. He will have a jury of twelve people to help him. The jurors will be just ordinary guys or gals who know nothing about the law. The judge will explain what he expects of them before and after they hear the evidence. The case might take two days or two months. The judge will send them off to make a decision. . ."

Bert hesitated, so I said, "So?"

Bert continued: "So if those jurors—who have no special training in law—come back into the courtroom and seven of them have decided 'guilty' and five voted 'innocent' the judge will blow his stack. He will chase them back into the jury room until they can agree on a verdict."

"So," I said again.

"So why can't our legal elite follow the same rules as the rest of the unwashed masses. Those old duffers should go right back into a huddle and stay there until they can reach a proper decision—until they can agree. If they can't do that, let them resign."

"Oh," I said as Bert rang off.

Socrates Expounds on Pornography

When I heard Bert's voice on the phone before breakfast, I muttered, "Now what," and reached for a pad and pen.

"What got you up so early? Must be six o'clock in Alberta."

"Been awake half the night, and the more I tossed and turned, the madder I got," Bert explained.

"What brought that on," I asked, knowing nothing could stop him from telling me anyway.

"I went to a high-school play last night. My neighbour's daughter, Laura, had a part. She's 15, sharp, and very pretty. Makes me wish I'd got married and had a daughter of my own."

"Bert, you're always wanting to adopt some young person or other."

Bert ignored me and stuck to his theme: "Got back from the school and stuck my nose into Walter's cafe. Place was empty except for Walter in the kitchen, Sheri his teenage daughter waitressing out front, and four young bucks in a rear booth. I noticed two of them ogling Sheri. Concerned, I stepped back to say hello. They brushed me off, so I walked on, but not before I got an eyeful of the magazines they had spread on the table. Rank, rotten pornography!"

"What did you do about it?" I asked.

"What could I do? It's legal. I didn't worry about Sheri; Walter has a very pretty daughter, but he also has a black belt. I went home to bed and landed right in the middle of a nightmare. I awoke in a cold sweat, seeing rotating visions of

Laura and Sheri, the four porno freaks in the cafe, and Paul Bernardo doing his thing on a video tape. I'd heard that Bernardo considered the girls nothing more than props for his activities. That made me wonder what it would take to push unstable men from porno magazines to living props.

"I didn't sleep much after that. I fretted and stewed and got madder and madder. I thought about all the do-gooders I had heard insisting that the disturbed, the criminals, and the abusers are all products of our society. They got that way because someone abused or deprived them. The same fuzzy thinkers insist that freedom of speech is so important that we can't take action to restrict pornography in our society. So out of one side of their mouths they blame vile practices on society, and out of the other side they condone corruption with pornography. And the people who live in mortal danger are those with little defence like Laura and Sheri!"

To slow Bert's tirade, I jumped in with a question: "Pornography certainly demeans women, but can anyone prove it actually promotes abuse?"

Bert snorted, "People today always want proof, by which they mean scientific evidence. They forget that great minds like Socrates used logic to arrive at truth. Try this for logic: if it is true pornography can titillate or sexually arouse a normal man, it must follow that pornography can drive an over-sexed or unstable or evil man into abuse or perversion."

I jumped in again, "Did you say the word evil? I thought you were agnostic."

"Yes I said evil. There isn't a better word to describe anyone who would harm Laura or Sheri."

"Bert, no one has harmed Laura or Sheri. But I get the point. So why are you sounding off at me?"

"Because you write a column and I don't. And I can hear your pencil scraping the pad."

"I hear you Socrates," I said in parting.

Democracy Looks Like a Milking Stool

Bert's laugh rattled from the telephone as he recalled an incident from our childhood: "Remember the day I came to your place to help with the milking? We used to argue the merits of single-legged, three-legged, and four-legged milking stools. You had invented a two-legged stool made from an apple crate and gave it to me to try. The stool was supposed to allow the milker to rock back and forth, but stay steady sideways. But one leg broke on the rickety thing when I tried to milk the old red cow."

"The stool broke," I cut in, "because you hit Old Red with it and cracked the leg. Later, when the cow kicked at you, you ducked, and the stool collapsed."

Bert snorted, "Have it your own way. The point is I fell face first into the manure gutter that you hadn't bothered to clean."

I laughed, but remembered I hadn't even snickered at the time—Bert outweighed me by 30 pounds. We rang off still laughing.

A week later a letter arrived from Bert, continuing the conversation. In it he said: "The two-legged stool makes a good illustration of modern democracy. The first leg speaks of representative government. If the majority doesn't rule, we have no democracy. The second leg gives voice to individuals—call it freedom of speech; without it we can't have full democracy. Of course the system doesn't always work well; typically, the two legs try to block sideways movement. Recent years in Ontario have demonstrated that curiosity. First the province tried to shift to the left under Bob Rae; now it's pushing to the right under Mike Harris—in both cases putting a lot of tension on the leg of free speech."

Bert's letter shifted from metaphor to political commentary: "As I listen to voices raised against government policy, I wonder how one can know if they really speak for minorities. I suspect most protest comes from organized pressure groups with agendas of their own. I'll give you examples.

"When your Harris government repealed NDP labour legislation, union leaders cried loudly and staged a job action. But I don't think most union members joined in, so I wondered if the labour leaders had planned the action to protect their own position and power.

"Then I read that Ontario lawyers began to protest changes to legal aid on behalf of their clients who used the service. They even began legal action. Typical, most trades or professions would strike, but lawyers sue! I wondered if they really feared the imminent death of a cash cow.

"Here in Alberta, the government put the squeeze on health services, so medical personnel cried out on behalf of patients, citing the erosion of services. But when they found their jobs on the line, they went on strike—making me question their real motivation.

"When a government or police force takes action against pornography in art, print, video, or the Internet, another group with a vested interest cries out on behalf of free speech. Take a look next time to see who yells 'censorship.' Usually it's your fellow writers who fear losing sales for the garbage they write."

That line made me mutter, "Bert, you're hitting below the belt."

Bert's letter concluded: "All groups have a right to free speech. But they should identify their true purposes or declare a conflict of interest and shut up. That would help the two-legged stool of democracy work better. And we the taxpayers wouldn't so often get our faces pushed into the cow manure."

Cherishing memories of Bert's dung-covered face, I placed his letter beside my computer and began to write.

Can Men Learn to Love?

Rarely, as a male of the species, has emotion struck me dumb. It has happened: once when I held my first newborn son; once on a snow-covered prairie watching a flock of Canada geese; and again when I saw the Taj Mahal. To my embarrassment, it happened again—only this time Anna saw it—a woman viewed this male's emotional crisis.

My friend Bert moved to Alberta about eight months ago. I admit I have missed him. Just days ago, a rap sounded at the apartment door—I beat Anna to it and pulled it open without first looking through the peephole. Bert walked in carrying an old suitcase. I stood there with my eyes bugging out; I couldn't say a word.

Anna greeted Bert as he pulled off his coat. He just grinned at me, but still I couldn't speak. Eventually, he said, "Well, I'm here! Sorry I didn't let you know."

I opened my mouth but words choked inside, so I stepped forward and threw my arms around him. My eyes got wet. When we stepped apart, Bert reached up with one finger, knocked a tear from my cheek, and said, "Hmmmm."

I finally spoke, "What are you doing here?"

"I needed to check on my property," he answered. "In fact, I must run up there now. Can you put me up tonight?"

"We can." Anna said. "And if you can get back by six we'll feed you."

Bert looked at his watch and said, "I'll be here."

He disappeared as quickly as he came. I turned toward my computer, but stopped as Anna challenged: "In forty years, I've never seen you guys act like that! You must really love him."

"Love him! Love that ornery, old coot? No one but his mother could love him," I snorted and quickly left the room.

Back at my desk, I stewed about that. I definitely loved my mother and sister. No question that I love my wife. I will confess to loving my sons and daughters-in-law—and everyone loves grandchildren. I even admit to a strong feeling of affection for some young women who, over the years, have taken the place of the daughters I never had. But love for another man? Hardly the right word to describe the relationship between two post-middle-age, traditional males.

Six o'clock came and went, but no Bert. A snowstorm raged outside; things looked bad. By eight o'clock my stomach had knotted up. Then came a knock, and Bert once again stood in our living room, this time shaking snow from his clothing.

"Where have you been?" I demanded. "You're two hours overdue! I imagined you stuck in a snowbank, injured in an accident, or even dead!"

He gave me a disdainful look, and said, "I was stuck, but I dug myself out. Not that you likely cared. If you'd driven five minutes down the road, you could have helped me."

"Why didn't you call? I would have come."

Bert shook his big head: "Didn't want to bother you—an old duffer like you would likely die doing all that shovelling."

"Old! Look whose talking. You shouldn't be digging with that bum ticker. I'll bet some cute little gal came along and dug you out."

Bert glared at me and said, "I'm hungry; let's eat."

I drank tea as he ate silently. I thought, "Thank goodness that snowstorm intervened so we could get back to a proper male-to-male relationship.

Then I glanced at Anna, and did what many couples can do after forty years, I read her mind: "Men are weird about affection. They deny it, hide it in bizarre language, even fight over it. No wonder women can't understand them; they can't even understand themselves."

Enjoying the Staff of Life

"That man is richest whose pleasures are the cheapest"— Thoreau.

Three sharp raps brought me bolt upright at six one morning. With the confusion of a sleep-encrusted mind, and the clumsiness of aging joints, I blundered to the apartment door. One look through the peephole snapped body and mind back to fighting trim. I could see nothing!

I didn't need to see anything because my fertile imagination auto-shifted into overdrive. I pictured a Chicago gangster with fedora pulled low and gat in hand, crouching just out of sight. I rejected that and conjured up a biker, wearing leathers and holding a chain, ready to strike from the shadows when I opened the door. That didn't make sense either. Maybe the landlord's wife had knocked to ask me to move my car for snow removal. At six? I rejected that idea too and returned to bed, but not before I noted the smell—a very pleasant smell—a neighbour making toast?

In bed as I pondered the smell, Bert came to mind. He had once worked in a bakery and would come by with fresh loaves. "That's it!" I thought. "Fresh baked bread."

An hour later I got up, passing the door on my way to the kitchen, and again smelled fresh-baked bread. I opened the door to check the hallway and found a paper bag with the words multi-grain scrawled across it. I brought it in and discovered a beautiful loaf of bread. Anna and I pigged out on it, finishing it all by the next day. But no one could tell us the origin of the mystery loaf.

Later that week Anna came home from shopping and said: "Now that Bert's back, I keep seeing him—today at the bulk store. He grinned and chatted away. I've never seen him so happy and pleased with himself."

"He's a lousy cook," I remarked. "So what did he buy?"

"He acted funny—kept his purchase hidden," she retorted.

The following morning the events of a few days earlier repeated. This time I did get to the door more quickly, opened it on the safety chain, and saw a shadow vanish from sight. I also saw a paper bag, marked with the words, 'Italian herb.' Anna sagely said, "Someone has a new breadmaker."

We ate half by noon, keeping the rest for the company we expected that night: Bert. When Bert arrived, he acted like a teenager who had just discovered girls, or an oldster who had won a lottery. He grinned, laughed, told jokes, and acted out of character. I hadn't see him like that for decades. When he sat at the table, he picked up a slice of Italian herb bread, sniffed it, and said, "What an odd smell for bread."

That's when the light came on—the early morning mystery visitor, Bert at the bulk store, Bert's strange behaviour. I said, "Italian herb smells that way. But it's not the smell that worries me. I just wonder if you get enough to eat when you keep giving away the output of your new breadmaker."

Bert looked stunned for a moment, then grinned: "I have never enjoyed anything more than that breadmaker. No new car, gun, or fishing rod can give a person more pleasure.

We bought one the next day. Bert and Thoreau were right, but there is a down side. As a slender, young female friend said, "Everybody I know who bought a breadmaker got fat."

Bert Does his Research

Bert dropped the pile of newspapers and magazines onto my table and, with a wry grin, said, "There it is. Everything you need to know to get inside Mike Harris's head."

Bert once lived in a little town in central Alberta. Back before television and VCRs, paved roads, and post-secondary education brought information about the world to local residents, Bert had a pipeline to knowledge. Bert read books, newspapers, magazines, trade publications, government documents, and manufacturers' sales and technical information. Although Bert never studied formally beyond grade 10, before he got out of his teens, the community started coming to him for insight and answers.

So it shouldn't have surprised me to see him still reading and pontificating forty years later. As I contemplated the stack of journals, Bert usurped my green chair, tipped it back to a comfortable, near-horizontal position, and stared toward the ceiling.

As I sat in a straight-back chair at the table and began leafing through the magazines and papers, Bert said, "It's all there. If all the demonstrators and whiners—be they doctors, nurses, teachers, factory workers, or bureaucrats—would read that they would have the answers. A much different answer from the me-first, spend-ourselves-into-bankruptcy, suck-future-generations-dry doctrine they now advocate."

Shuddering at Bert's invective, I said, "So," and waited.

"It's all in writing," Bert continued. "Whatever problems we have, someone else has already been there and learned. New Zealand, one of the world's earliest welfare states, teetered on bankruptcy in the mid-eighties. Every working individual actually supported another person and his or her descendants through welfare payments and subsidies. Government departments and business alike depended on subsidies and over-taxation to function. Most of them lost any real concept of efficiency, production, or personal responsibility."

"So what did they do," I prompted.

"They cut taxes, reduced the civil service by sixty percent, cut welfare, eliminated subsidies to farmers and industry, increased user fees, and legislated away some of the power of unions. Now unemployment is down to about six percent, the national debt is down, and economic growth is one of the greatest in the industrialized world. And the people are better off, better motivated."

"How," I asked, "do you cut the civil service and maintain important services like classroom education?"

Bert paused only for a moment, then said, "Be creative. For example, do what they do in Japan. There, students spend 15 to 30 minutes each day cleaning the school—scrubbing the toilets, sweeping the floors, and washing graffiti off the walls. In fact when kids write graffiti, they use pencils. They know they'll later clean it off. The students learn personal responsibility while saving bags of money by doing janitorial work."

I frowned: "But I have heard negative things about Japanese schools."

Bert sighed heavily: "That's the point! Be creative. Take the worthwhile ideas and ignore the bad ones. The Harris detractors don't know these things, because most of them are functionally illiterate. They get most of their knowledge from 15-second news bites on television. They don't take time to read and learn about the real world outside the boob tube."

With that Bert prepared to leave. I scooped up his magazines and loaded them in his arms. "Don't you want to read these?" he asked, dumfounded.

"Nope. Bert, as long as I have friends like you, I don't need to read."

"Illiterate cretin," Bert muttered, as he scowled, and stomped out the door.

Checking out the Internet

I had just snuggled down into my green chair when someone knocked on the apartment door. Tempted not to answer, I crept up to the door and looked through the peephole. I could see nothing but a huge cardboard carton. "Delivery man at the wrong address," I muttered as I snapped back the bolt and opened the door.

The big box pushed past me and headed straight for the dining-room table, propelled by none other than Bert, one eye peaking out from behind. "My new computer," he mumbled against the back of the box. "I want you to help me set it up. I'll go back to the truck for the rest of it."

Bert made three more trips, eventually piling two middle-sized boxes beside the first. He tossed three or four small, brightly-coloured cartons on my green chair. Seeing me shudder, he said, "That's software. It won't hurt your precious chair."

Without further comment he produced a pocketknife and began slitting open the packing tape. Knowing his take-over style, I stood by and watched. The large box gave birth to a name-brand pentium computer and keyboard. A monitor and printer appeared from the other boxes. I looked at neatly-coiled cables, and said, "I don't know much about computers."

"You know more than I do. You've had one for ten years."

I shrugged. As we assembled the components, Bert explained what had brought on this latest acquisition: "You know I read and study a lot. I thought it was time to get modern and get on the internet, on the Worldwide Web. I spend hours searching through the library and bookstores. This way I'll get information off the net and save time and gas."

We worked all afternoon assembling the new toy and loading software. Contrary to normal experience with new computers, everything worked. We even plugged it into the phone line and accessed the internet. Bert stayed through the evening while we surfed the internet, visiting sites, malls, and home pages around the world. At 10 o'clock he packed up the computer and went home.

I didn't see Bert for another month. Every time I called his number, I got a busy signal. I guessed he had become a true computer nerd, spending every moment on the internet. I sent two messages by e-mail and received short, curt responses. I missed seeing his face and hearing his voice. He appeared unannounced at my door one evening with a large, old book tucked under his arm. He looked so bleary-eyed and tired, I ushered him to my green chair, seating myself on a straight-back.

"I sold it," he said. "Computers grip you like a narcotic, so I quit cold turkey. I've gone back to books." Handing me the book, he continued, "Thought you might find this Edersheim interesting. I found it in a used-book store."

I took the book, but didn't open it. "What happened to the computer?" I asked.

"I missed books. I missed the library. I missed chatting with real people like librarians and bookstore clerks. I spent so much time at the computer browsing the world that my backside hurt, my fingers went arthritic, my wrists developed carpal tunnel syndrome, and my heart ached for my friends and neighbours. I longed to sit on my back porch and read a book, or walk down a country lane with one under my arm. I missed smelling the musty odour of old books and flipping through yellowed pages."

I nodded in understanding as I fondled the cloth cover of Edersheim. I have never lovingly caressed a computer.

Defining the Family

The Slippery Slope to Laughter

In my late teens I owned an Austin car in partnership with my mother. Since she owned part of it she expected transportation to shops, on visits to friends, to meetings, to church, and on the occasional joy ride. I obliged; it's a good business practice to keep your minority investors happy. One muddy day in the fall, I parked on the edge of the street at the base of a waist-high, sloping embankment in front of the house. I saw her exit by the front door and head for the car by angling across the wet front lawn.

I had given her lots to complain about. I had not parked at the steps coming down the slope. Neither did I climb from the car to help the lady—then in her late fifties—negotiate the slope. Nor did I think to open the car door. I just sat and waited, sure that one with such a fiercely independent streak needed and wanted no help.

She could have griped about the muddy roadside in front of our rented cottage, or about the lack of a sidewalk. She might even have blamed the weatherman—or God—for the rotten weather on the day of her planned outing. However, she had overcome too many major obstacles in life to pout over trivialities.

I watched her approach the embankment across the lawn, then dropped back into my teenage reverie; at that time I had a crush on a young lady who sang in the Leslie Bell Singers on the fledgling CBC television service. What young person would waste time worrying about a parent when one had access to mental visions like that?

I snapped out of my reverie when I realized Mother had vanished. She should be getting into the car, but had disappeared from the front lawn as if a fiery chariot from heaven had snatched her away. I sat puzzled for a moment, but quickly became alarmed when I heard a sobbing or choking sound. I leaned across the narrow car and threw the passenger door open. From the vantage point of that near-horizontal position, I looked down over the door sill directly into Mother's face. Only her head and shoulders protruded from under the car. Losing her footing on the slope, she had tobogganed through the mud and slush, coming to a stop beneath the car.

Her head and shoulders shook with convulsions of laughter. To her this was the funniest thing that had happened in years. She continued to laugh even when I pulled and tugged, trying to free her ample body from the grip of the transmission and exhaust system. She howled with glee when I landed beside her in the mud. Neighbours peeked at us from behind curtained windows. Thankfully, they neither offered help nor intruded on a memorable time of joy for mother and son. Eventually I hauled her free and we returned to the house to clean up and prepare for a new start.

For the rest of her life, Mother continued to temper times of unhappiness with a great deal of laughter. When I want to gripe and complain I remember an Austin car, a slippery slope, and a mud-covered pair howling and grappling in the muck at the roadside; I remember a legacy of laughter.

Flight out of Danger

I like to think I am a good storyteller. Certainly I have known some great ones over the years, both personally and through the media. We all face the same problem with storytellers: how do we know when to believe them?

From about age seven I read Gregory Clark's column in
the Star Weekly and believed every word he wrote. It took
many years before I learned to judge when he strayed from
fact and drifted into fantasy and whimsy. Usually, it's easier
when the storyteller exercises his craft face to face: you can
watch for the averted look, the gleam in the eye, or the sly
grin. I had one of those encounters a few weeks back.

I sat across the desk from Ken in his office in a hanger at
Pearson International Airport. Ken, sometimes for business,
sometimes for pleasure, flies around in a single-engine Piper
Comanche. I always wanted to learn to fly, so I am an easy
mark for airplane stories. "Tell me," I asked him, "about your
trip in the Comanche down to Freeport."

"We didn't go to Freeport. We went to Marsh Harbour in
the Bahamas," he answered. Before he could continue, the
roar of a Garrett turbo-prop engine drowned out our
conversation. We simply sat and looked at each other until the
air ambulance had left the apron and taxied toward the
runway.

As though nothing had happened, Ken continued, "It took
us three days to get there. Should have taken only nine and a
half hours, but the weather kept grounding us. When we
arrived, we liked Marsh Harbour so much, we stayed there
rather than visit other islands. We went swimming and diving
and then came home."

"Was that all? Surely something interesting must have
happened," I prodded.

He shrugged and said, "Pretty routine flight, except for
the bad weather going down—not much better coming back."

I tried again: "Nothing exciting, like engine failure, or
getting lost over the ocean or something?"

He leaned back in his chair, stared at the ceiling, and
answered, "Actually something did happen on the way back
between Marsh Harbour and Fort Pierce in Florida. Our
course took us over 90 miles of ocean—through the corner of

the infamous Bermuda Triangle."

Now he was getting somewhere. I had read about that section of the Atlantic. The lore of the sea and the air tell of many strange happenings there—ships and squadrons of airplanes vanishing forever. Some who sailed or flew successfully through the Bermuda Triangle tell of compass and equipment failures and other inexplicable happenings. Ken certainly had my attention.

He continued: "We flew over Freeport, then across the ocean toward Fort Pierce. We hadn't gone far when I noticed the ADF wouldn't work. That device helps to navigate by indicating the direction to radio stations. I didn't think much of it until the cylinder-head temperature gauge failed. That instrument works much like the engine temperature gauge on your car."

"What did you think then?" I asked.

Ken just grinned and said, "I pointed out the failures and said to the other guys in the plane, 'Hey, cool! We're in the Bermuda Triangle, and it's happening.' A moment later the gauge that indicates exhaust-gas temperature quit working. It's critical in adjusting the fuel mixture. Fortunately, I can do that by engine sound. Next we lost our number two VOR. A VOR indicates the plane's position relative to a navigational station. Most pilots navigate using a VOR. Fortunately, we still had another VOR and a magnetic compass. In any case, if we kept going west, we'd come to Florida."

"Is that all? What happened next?" I asked, glued to the edge of my chair.

"Nothing, really. Five minutes out of Fort Pierce, all the needles jumped back into place. Everything worked fine all the way back to Toronto."

I stared at Ken. Was he stringing me along—just another pilot adding to the lore of the Bermuda triangle? No, I had to believe every word of this story. You see, I haven't told you one important fact—Ken is my son.

When the Old Serpent Gives Orders

Plato said of boys: ". . . of all wild beasts, the most difficult to handle." Tell us about it Plato! We raised four of them.

Two decades ago in South Africa we had no money, four active sons, and a desire to stay on good terms with our neighbours. One day two of the boys entertained themselves by bouncing green apricots off a neighbour's tin roof. We scolded the boys and mollified the hostile neighbour.

A few days later, another neighbour said accusingly, "The day after your kids were throwing things, I found 17 broken windows in my greenhouse roof."

I gulped, picturing money flying from my meagre food and clothing budget and onto my neighbour's roof. "But I don't think your boys actually did it," he continued. "We had a bad storm that night."

I quizzed the boys, heard their denials, and assured the neighbour that my sons would never ever commit such a crime.

Then back in Canada ten years later my youngest son, Ken, told the following story at a party—I heard it secondhand. Let me warn you, Ken has his father's gift of storytelling, but you can believe the essentials.

Ken told it this way: One day in South Africa, I saw a juicy pomegranate hanging from a branch just above the neighbour's greenhouse. I licked my lips in anticipation, but hesitated. Then I heard a noise in the grass at my feet. Looking down I saw a small snake. The snake hissed and said, "Go and get it."

"No," I answered, "that would be stealing. And besides, I'm not supposed to climb on the wall and certainly not on the greenhouse."

"Go and get it," ordered the snake. "You won't get into trouble."

Starting toward the wall, I could almost taste the fruit, but I stopped again. The snake hissed once more and said, "Go, go, go!"

I went. I scampered to the top of the brick wall. From there stretching before me, I saw panes of glass framed by metal strips. I stepped onto the metal frame at the edge of the glass roof. After balancing there for a moment, I began picking my way slowly toward the middle and the pomegranate, placing my feet carefully on the thin metal frames. In a moment, the fruit hung just above my head. By standing with one foot on each side of a pane, I could just about reach the red juicy ball. I stretched to full height, raised up on tip toes and grabbed the pomegranate.

As my fingers closed, I turned for the return journey, but lost my balance and landed one foot in the middle of a pane. Cracks exploded in all directions. Frightened that I might fall through, I stepped to the next pane with the same results. Terrified, I ran for the edge—each step smashing a glass pane—leaped from the roof, and went into hiding.

There Ken ended his story. He has no idea what happened to the pomegranate.

Ten years after publicly telling that story, Ken, happily married, has a beautiful daughter, two proud parents, and a key position with an air transport company. Today, only one thing hints at his "adventurous" childhood: his mother's and my grey hair.

Do you have one of those "wild beasts" in your family, testing your patience, keeping you awake at night? Take heart, in another ten or twenty years, you may burst with pride and join us in saying, "It really was worth it all."

When a Robin, a Frog, and a Princess Speak

Why do so many people have difficulty defining the family? If we really want to understand, maybe we should use fewer words and pay more attention to the living examples all around us.

"Watch that baby Robin," I commanded Anna one morning. She responded by carefully parting the slats and looking into a glorious spring morning.

As we watched, Dad Robin left the side of the baby and sped across the packed earth of the roadway. He moved with frantic hops, almost as if his feet burned on a hot surface. At our lawn he stopped, cocked his head to listen, then struck downward to begin a life and death tug-of-war with an earth worm. The worm lost. Dad rushed back to baby and jammed the wiggling meal into the youngster's mouth where it disappeared in one gulp.

Noticing that the tiny, speckled body didn't seem to have tail feathers, I said, "It can't fly. Either a car will run over it or a cat will kill it." As we watched a ginger-coloured head peeked from tall grass beneath a tree. Two kilograms of finely-tuned muscle, claw, and fang, eased from the cover and began a belly-crawl of horror toward the helpless baby. Morris, the neighbour's orange cat, in answer to primal instinct, stiffened his steel-like muscles to make the final spring.

"Cheep, cheep," warned Dad robin. The baby took a running leap into the air, its tiny wings a blur of motion. Its body rocked back and forth as its puny tail feathers fought for control. Seconds later it crash-landed in the safety of a tree. Morris hurled cat curses after his lost prey then slinked away in search of an easier kill.

A few days later, we sat in a restaurant across from a blue-eyed, blond frog, age three and a half. Actually, Julie just looked like a frog that day. She had attended a birthday party earlier and had kept the green face paint that attracted attention wherever she went. She accepted attention from family and strangers and reacted by adopting the manner of a celebrity.

"Watch that kid," I said to Anna as Julie excused herself from the table. Before climbing from her chair, she leaned over to cousin Peter, age two, and gave him a kiss. Before our eyes, Julie the frog turned into Julie the politician, kissing his head and patting him on the shoulder. After reaching the floor, the frog became a diplomat, and marched to the head of the table. There she bowed low and said serious goodbyes to Uncle and Aunt.

Progressing along the table, Julie next stopped opposite Grandma and Grandpa. In the twinkling of an eye, frog changed to royalty. Julie curtsied, waved in true regal fashion, and smiled with her eyes. A princess needs to guard against overemoting in public. With a bow and a sweep of an arm she advanced toward Mom. In three short steps princess became starlet, dancing a pirouette in front of her mother. With each spin she tossed off flirtatious kisses, first to Mom, next to the gathered family, then to total strangers at the next table.

The other restaurant guests stopped eating and turned toward the frog that had become princess and starlet. One lady leaned from her chair six tables away, to watch the impromptu floor show, her food forgotten. A waiter, serving tray at shoulder height, stopped and stared, food and customers forgotten.

Julie had saved the best for last. She stopped before her dad, her hero, her protector, the love of her life, and exploded into a brilliant smile. She bowed, she waved, she danced and sang out, "G'bye Dad, g'bye, g'bye, g'bye."

Embarrassed by the public attention, her hero, protector, and love of her life, said, "Julie, for goodness sake, you're only going to the washroom!"

How Sisters Demonstrate Love

Often words won't work in circumstances where other methods of communication come through loud and clear. My assignment, while staying with an African family on the edge of the Great Rift Valley, required that I examine communication processes among the Kikuyu people.

Early Sunday I stood beside an African house on the very edge of the valley. An early-morning mist had filled that great gash in the earth's surface with cottony whiteness and restricted my vision to about 100 metres. I should have experienced an awesome sense of stillness and solitude, but a radio clamoured for attention from the house on the next tiny farm. The radio played a hymn with words in English.

The hymn ended and the distinctive voice of an American evangelist rang out loud and clear. "What," I asked, "is he doing here? Few people here speak English, and none speak his drawling dialect."

Suddenly, someone changed stations, readjusting to one carrying orchestral music. I realized that I had more data for my thesis. The preacher paid good money for air time, but forgot an important communication principle: if the intended target of a message doesn't receive it, no communication takes place. Typical of many North Americans, he considered English a universal language.

Then I thought of the marvellous time of communication

I had enjoyed the day before. With my guide, Peter, I had visited a neighbour family for tea. The princess-like daughter of that home had returned for a visit after living for years in England, bringing with her the clothes and look of success.

We passed through a gateway in a palisade surrounding two tiny houses. A man and a woman, looking over a half door in one residence, directed us to the other. We walked carefully through the yard, sidestepping chickens and other farm creatures, and called out at the doorway of the second house.

We entered on invitation, ducking low to avoid the smoke—Kikuyu houses have no chimney. I sat on a low, three-legged stool near the fire with Peter beside me. Most of the others, sitting on the floor, chatted with each other in Kikuyu. The mother, opposite me across the fire, rooted in the hot ashes and found a baked potato, which she pushed to me with her fire stick. A neighbour lady, who arrived a few minutes later, sat beside the mother. Peter interpreted just enough to keep me in total confusion.

However, the scene that really caught and held my attention, appeared just to my left—you guessed it, the "princess." She wore a dress just as fashionable and spotless as the one she wore the day before when she stepped off the bus. She had abandoned her leather shoes and, like her sister at her side, had bare feet. Yes, the princess had a sister—a 10-year-old wearing a well-worn dress, the dust and dirt of the farmyard clinging to her in the fashion of any child who enjoys the outdoors.

They both sat on a mat on the floor. Little sister cuddled against big sister as though she had found a long-lost treasure. Big sister wrapped one arm about little sister in a pose that said, "I love you; you belong to me." Simplicity and elegance held each other in an embrace that ignored the hard floor, the dust and dirt, the smoky room, and the presence of a stranger.

The man and woman from the first house entered and sat

with the others across the fire. I supposed him the father of
the princess, but something seemed wrong; something that I
couldn't quite grasp clashed with my Canadian culture.

We drank tea, I finished my potato, and we took our
leave. As we walked slowly back, Peter asked, "Did you
figure it out?"

"No," I said. "Something seemed different, but I'm not
sure what."

Peter put the pieces together for me, explaining that the
man had two wives and, therefore, two houses. The princess
was the daughter of his first wife, and the little sister
belonged to the second wife. The first wife occupied the
house we visited.

Without the language, and without much understanding of
the culture, a powerful message of love had reached out and
touched me. It did so in circumstances in which my Canadian
upbringing had prepared me to expect only dissension and
unhappiness.

When Kinfolk Intervene

If they hadn't torn down the old farmhouse, I could still visit
the very spot where my "snivelling post" stood. The old shaft
had once anchored the swinging side of a gate. But the gate
had long gone and the old pine stake stood barren and alone
at the north-west corner of the entry to the windblown,
clapboard dwelling.

I visited that post often in my pre-school days. With one
arm wrapped around it, I would whine, and cry, and snivel,
and pour out tales of woe. Why did I pick that post as the
object of my grief and sorrow? Possibly because it had lost its
purpose and stood forlorn and useless, and so I saw it as a

fellow traveller on the road to self-pity and misery. More
likely it marked a halfway point between the security of the
house and the terrors that must surely lurk just beyond in the
empty prairie landscape. Whatever the reason, I arrived often
to grip its shredded bark, and whine, and howl, and cry out
my protests against a cruel and unfair world.

Goodness knows I had plenty to complain about. No one
bought me any new toys, only used ones at Christmas and
birthdays. All my clothes came as hand-me-downs from my
older brother and neighbours. I tasted candy only at Christmas
and never had spending money on the rare times we visited
town. My big brother picked on me, and my father spent most
of his time in the hospital.

Then in one magic moment, it all changed. My
circumstances didn't alter, if anything they worsened, but my
attitude toward them underwent a revolution. My hero, Jess,
on an unexpected visit appeared around the corner as I clung
to my snivelling post and sent a mighty howl heavenward.
Jess, who had married my cousin Emily, acted as my
substitute dad.

Jess came to a halt at the sight of this small boy clinging
to a post and wailing loudly. This quiet man of few words,
but capable of great depth and understanding, stood and stared
and gathered his thoughts. He did not know if inward or
outward pain had provoked the outburst; indeed I can no
longer recall the cause.

Jess reached out and touched me with his voice; men
rarely used physical contact to communicate tenderness back
then. "Lad," he said quietly, "whatever has hurt you can't be
all that bad. Why not save all that crying, and noise, and
energy for some time when you really need it?"

I don't know if Jess's unexpected appearance, tender
words, or common sense did it, but something at that moment
changed me. I won't claim I never again whined or
complained about my lot in life, but Jess's intervention meant

I did a lot less of it than I might have.

Today when I hear the various commentators on the world scene—the economists and political pundits, the expert and the inept—whining about government or lack of government, I react. My first response is to get mad and tell them to shut up and do something positive to help the situation instead of exacerbating it with noisy complaining.

But after a moment's thought, I feel sorry for them. I realize that they in their pre-school days, didn't have a poor, prairie dirt-farmer to challenge them to abandon their "snivelling post" and redirect their energies, to save their strength for the real issues and emergencies of life—to make a difference and not just a noise.

A Prairie Wind Can't Loosen the Family Tie

The best present I ever received as a youngster arrived 15 days after Christmas.

But first, a detour. In the summer of 1947, the dust storms that had devastated the prairies in the 1930s still returned for occasional assaults on central Alberta. An eerie moaning sound warned us of an impending attack. My brother heard it first, and rushed around the machine shed for a clear view of the western horizon. A huge, black, earth-bound cloud rolled toward our farmstead. Harry pivoted and raced toward the barn, yelling at the top of his voice: "Dust storm! Dust storm!"

All of us sprang into action. While Harry wrestled the big sliding barn doors shut, I sped to the chicken house. Chicken's often show more sense than the epithet "bird brain" suggests. Most of them had spotted the approaching terror and scurried into the protection of the henhouse. I chased the stragglers in, closed the door, and joined Harry who had now returned to the machine shed. We quickly closed the big doors, then surveyed the barnyard for loose items that would race before the wind.

Meanwhile, Mother hurried about the house closing windows. She had trained us in quick response, and concerned herself only with her responsibilities, knowing we would take care of ours. Remembering the clothes on the line, she grabbed a basket and did a Dagwood Bumstead run out the back door. For once Harry and I had moved faster, stripped off the laundry, and met her on the way out. Flying arms and legs, scattered shirts and underwear, and peals of laughter added a lighter note to a serious situation.

I grabbed a pillowcase from the teeth of the wind and dashed into the house. Mother turned to me, "Isn't Shirley with you? She should be back from visiting Doreen."

All of us ran back out of the house into the increasing wind to look along the road as it crossed the coulee bottom and climbed the rise toward the neighbour's place. Through the gathering gloom we saw a tiny wind-buffeted figure running down the slope. She still had a half mile between her and safety. "She'll be terrified," Mother said matter-of-factly.

Before anyone could say another word, and because we all knew our responsibilities, I took off at a full run. My brother, older, but heavier and with a heart problem, should not—indeed could not—run any distance. I, who rarely had a working bicycle or a rideable horse, had learned to run for miles on end.

As the sky grew darker, I dropped over the crest of the hill, raced past the well on the coulee bottom, and entered the road. I caught only glimpses of Shirley's tiny form through the driving dust. The wind ripped at my clothes and pushed me toward the ditch. I had visions of it blowing Shirley into the ponds at the roadside. She broke into full view as we approached the culvert that drained the muskrat pond. Tears ran down her cheeks, mingling with the prairie dust that coated her face.

I will never forget the look of relief that pushed away fear as she caught her big brother's hand. It really wasn't such a big deal—just another little adventure that came with growing up on a prairie farm in the 1940s. But that magic moment sealed a brother-sister relationship that stands firm today.

What has all that to do with Christmas gifts? Just this: a few years before that storm and just 15 days after Christmas, Shirley had joined our family. And for two millennia, Christmas has focused on people, on family—not on material gifts.

Family Treasures in Cardboard

I discovered the old magazines before my ninth birthday. Someone had rolled them up, wrapped them with brown paper, and stored them—along with a cardboard box filled with newspaper clippings—on a basement shelf in our old farmhouse. I spirited everything to my second-floor room, closed the door, spread the clippings on my bed, and carefully unrolled the magazines. I soon realized I had found a treasure.

Buried in the newspaper clippings, I unearthed a tiny, hard-cover notebook. Small pencilled handwriting filled the pages. I could read almost any printed material, but handwriting confounded me. As I held the little book, a tingle ran up my arm and through my body. This must be the 'Boer War Diary' I had heard Mother mention—the commentary of a scout with the British army in South Africa. I battled again to read it, but gave up after deciphering only four words, "lost another horse today . . ." In my mind I heard the crack of a rifle shot and saw the horse fall as the scout rolled into the protection of the scrub. I put the book away almost reverently; it would have to wait till my reading skills improved.

I turned to the yellowest of the clippings dating to the turn of the century. They told of the wins and records made by a British bicycle racer, dubbed the "Manchester Sizzler" who rode with a club called the Manchester Wheelers. My eyes grew larger as I read of 12-hour endurance tests and cross-country races.

Next I turned to the magazines. They proved to be sports magazines, published in England and dated 1907 to 1909. Some of them contained adventuresome accounts written by a former editor who had emigrated to western Canada. One entitled "On Board a Canadian Liner" recounted his experience travelling to Canada third class, or 'steerage' with his wife and four children. On leaving the ship at Halifax, they boarded a 'colonist train' bound for Alberta. The account finishes with the family arriving, by farm wagon, at a prairie homestead.

The rest of the clippings, written in the 1920s contained letters to the editor of a Canadian newspaper from an Alberta farmer on a world tour. He had sent reports from Egypt describing the wonder of the pyramids, from India picturing the beauty of the Taj Mahal, from Australia recounting visits with friends, and from Hawaii giving a detailed description of Honolulu. That one ended with an invitation to visit Hawaii and a pun: "Honolulu will honour you-you"

I carefully repacked every item and returned them to their basement shelf. Over the years I returned to the shoe box again and again. What I read excited me more than any library book for the soldier, cyclist, editor, writer, storyteller, homesteader, and world traveller were one person—my father.

At first I had a hard time identifying this hero with the aged man who occasionally visited from the hospital. Dad had remarried, had three more children spaced nearly 40 years behind the first family, then took ill after only six years of his new marriage. So I knew him best through his writing.

As I contemplate his story and mine, the power of words to influence amaze me. Without conscious thought, I have followed his example closely, recapitulating some of his varied careers, often standing where he stood. As a child, I barely knew him, but through his written words, I can feel his hand on my shoulder today.

Keep reading. Keep your kids reading. Video, computers, and the internet are tools or toys of a mere half century, but writing has influenced human experience and growth for five thousand years.

Unity and Diversity

A day or two after Christmas, Ken, my youngest son, arrived with his wife Anne and daughter Julie. Ken carried in a large framed illustration of some sort. He had a twinkle in his eye that put me on my guard. Youngest sons like to outfox their fathers—it has something to do with birth position, or pecking order, or something.

He positioned the frame on a chair, but I chose to ignore it, turning instead to Anne and Julie. And why not? Both are much prettier than Ken, and as for Julie—well you haven't seen a grandchild until you have met Julie. After hugs and kisses, I turned back to Ken, and influenced by the yuletide spirit, I hugged him. Then I looked at the framed picture.

I saw a multi-coloured, finely-detailed pattern. "It looks like yuppie wallpaper," I remarked—a comment designed to stir up the generation battle.

"No," he insisted, "it's an illusion. If you look at it carefully you can see another picture hidden in the background, a three-dimensional image."

Now I remembered. I have seen these things in shopping malls. Invariably people stand around them oohing and aahing and saying things like, "I see it; I see it," or "Oh, look, there it is—it's a mermaid!"

I have looked over their shoulders, seeing nothing but strange patterns. After a few minutes of screwing up my eyes, tilting my head, staring through glasses formed by looped fingers and thumbs, and going cross-eyed I have left with serious concern about the mental stability of my fellow human beings.

I tried all the same techniques on Ken's yuppie wallpaper, before saying, "You can't see anything in that."

"Yes I can, and so could you if you tried harder," he insisted.

I tried harder. Nothing.

"Try focusing on your reflection in the glass, and it will disappear and the hidden image will appear," he insisted.

I tried that until my eyes almost popped out. Nothing.

"There is no hidden picture. It's just a big hoax," I asserted.

Perplexed I took a few moments to reflect. I thought about differences and personal perception. Often members of our family see things in radically different ways. No matter how much we stare, study, or scrutinize we can't quite get the picture as they see it. Each of us looks from a different perspective, from a diverse background. All look through a unique set of filters coloured by age, intellectual, educational, cultural, and religious experience.

Yes, even within our initially Scots-English family, our four sons married girls who have introduced elements of Czech, Polish, Dutch, Ukrainian, and Irish culture. Just to accentuate the differences among us, five couples now represent five different church denominations. We have learned to live with difference and make the attendant tensions into points of growth. We will never see everything exactly the same way.

Now if we, and all modern families, can expand what we have learned and apply it to our community, our country, and our world we can begin to make greater contributions.

Just before Ken and family left, I took a last look at the "yuppie wallpaper." As I stared at my own reflection in the glass, it slowly faded away. The intricate patterns began to break up into three-dimensional layers, almost like cloud banks. A shadowy image began to materialize. I never saw all the detail that others claimed, but I could see it!

So hope for tolerance and growth still reigns in our diverse world—even for me.

Family Perspective from the Green Chair

Green symbolizes growth and life. Perhaps for that reason I prefer to work, think, and write in a green room.

Unfortunately, I no longer have a green room. However, I recently bought a comfortable, green reclining chair. As I sat in it and tried the various angles from upright to near horizontal, I noticed the symbolism of the different positions. From the upright I stared directly into the pale, unhealthy, unblinking eye of the television set. A simple movement of my right hand could bring it to life carrying the world with all its bumps and warts into my living room. I resisted the siren call of the remote control and tilted the chair full back.

From this position I stared upward. Now I could use the remote control of the mind to move my consciousness heavenward, shut out the noisy world, and muse on hundreds of things, real or imagined.

I moved the chair's control to the mid-position, the compromise setting, the place where too many of us spend our lives. From this position I said aloud, "Now I have joined the crowd the news media call the 'silent majority,'—those caught between two opinions."

I returned the chair to upright, but noticed the TV again and quickly rocked all the way back to the 'muse' position. I began to think about the influence television has on family life. A few years back, quite a few years ago, television presented a picture of families that modern critics love to ridicule. Many columnists, commentators, critics and a host of other self-appointed authorities claim families like those pictured in 'Leave it to Beaver' or 'Lassie' or even 'I Love Lucy' never existed except in the minds of idealists.

I remembered real families I had known way back before TV as I grew up in a one-parent home. The Vincett family, headed by one mother and one father, raised 12 kids, all of whom became good citizens. They lived in an old house, adding rooms as kids arrived. When I visited as a child, I experienced family life from their perspective: high adventure, hilarity, and close fellowship, although not without the tensions and rivalries that help build character.

I remembered also the Leif and Ellen Rossing family. At meal times Leif's presence commanded a discipline I had never seen anywhere else. No one reached for the next course until he did. Children spoke only when spoken to. It seemed stern or unreal until I saw the family at fun, gathered around the crokinole board or around Leif as he played his concertina. One day family discipline paid off; a farm accident severed one son's arm. He not only lived, but the small town doctor sewed the arm on years before medical people thought such a procedure possible. Without the discipline, speed, and cooperation of a closely-knit family, that could never have happened.

Those real families outclassed even the most idealistic 1950s television clans.

Next, I considered families portrayed in modern sitcoms and soaps. I rarely watch any for more than a few minutes. Most seem to feature double entendre, warped or perverted sex, crudeness, and bad taste.

No one has ever asked me to pick families as models to emulate. If someone did, I would compare the old, idealistic, TV families, the real families I have known and admired, and the modern TV versions. Frankly, the smut-oriented, broken, and injured families of modern TV wouldn't even get a consideration. Gosh, I hope I'm not alone with that viewpoint!

It's time to quit my musings from the green chair, shift to the vertical, turn on the TV, and watch Vana, Pat, and the wheel of fantasy and greed.

Time Travel in the Green Chair

Most of us enjoyed reading Calvin and Hobbes before that excellent strip disappeared from the comics. Calvin, the hyperactive brat, had a stuffed tiger, Hobbes, who became a living, almost-human tiger whenever he and Calvin were alone. Some of us actually identified with Calvin—not necessarily because of impish behaviour—but because we have kept our Hobbes; we have preserved our childhood imaginations.

I don't have a stuffed tiger, but I do own a stuffed green chair. I settled back in it before Christmas, pulled the recliner's shift lever to horizontal and stared at the ceiling. But only for a moment, for the shift-to-horizontal control also fires the retro rockets of imagination.

As my eyes closed, the chair whisked me across the miles and back through the decades to a prairie farmhouse. In a second-floor bedroom, I watched two Calvin-sized rascals waking on Christmas morning. As they popped their heads from under the covers, their eyes grew large, focusing on stockings stuffed with toys and goodies. For a moment they didn't move. Two little heads protruded from the covers, breath freezing in the ill-heated room. The heads turned toward each other, grinned, then bounced toward stockings hanging on the foot of the bed. Both retreated back under the covers to examine their loot. Cries of "a gun, I gotta gun!" "I got one too!" "candy and an orange!" "look, nuts!" and "I got crayons!" filtered through the piles of bedding.

After a moment, the smallest child reappeared, landed on his knees on the floor, and pulled a chamber pot from beneath the bed. Seconds later the larger boy threw back the covers, and with Christmas stocking under his arm and toy pistol in hand said, "Let's go down and see what Shirley got!"

"Wait for me!" yelled the other as he collected Santa's gifts. Both raced downstairs. Although the rule said, "Wash before you come down in the morning," neither took time to break the ice in the wash basin.

The parcels under the tree provided a wind-up train for each boy and a doll for Shirley. Mother said, "We've had a great Christmas because Aunt Elsie sent a box with things for all of us. The toy guns and trains belonged to her boys. Without Elsie's help it would have been a poor Christmas."

The green chair chugged ahead one year and jumped back to Ontario. It paused by a skinny tree in a city house on Christmas morning. The warm house had electric lights and inside plumbing. It even had a large radio playing Christmas carols. Two dispirited boys entered the scene. Each one, still in pyjamas dropped to the floor by the tree. The lower parts of each face appeared swollen. The youngest spoke: "Mom, why did we have to get mumps for Christmas?"

"I don't have an answer for that, but I am happy that Aunt Elsie is looking after Shirley. At least she didn't get the mumps. We should also thank God for our new home and my job, even though we have few presents to open this year. But by next Christmas Shirley will be home—we'll be four again."   And so I return to the present. Although we all idealize the past, many of us recall some pretty bleak holiday celebrations. We should remember them, expressing thanks for today's blessings. It's too late for this Christmas, but that shouldn't stop us from helping at any time those in need—then one day they too will look back with pleasure on times past.

Oh, you might like to know: Shirley rejoined the family and got the mumps for the next Christmas!

Aunt Harri Looks Ahead

Time to Move on

"Needed to get out of there," commented Aunt Harri from the back seat of our new car. We had used the new car as an excuse to coax her out for a ride. We said nothing, just continued driving along beautiful, tree-lined country roads. Unfortunately, our passenger's failing eyesight limited her enjoyment of the beauty about her.

Aunt Harri spoke again, quietly as though to herself: "It gets very difficult living in partial darkness, depending on others to go to the shops when I need things, and allowing others to launder my dirty clothes. My old, arthritic fingers battle to replace batteries in this tiny hearing aid. I eat food I don't like because someone puts it on my plate. I get short-tempered with those who help, and they respond in kind. And to top it off, there is a lot of abuse in an old folks' home."

A chill ran down my spine. "Abuse?" I questioned.

"Yes abuse. Not what you're thinking. Most of the workers treat us well. It's the other way around—many of the residents abuse the staff. Some old and crotchety folks take it out on those near them. One old fellow strikes out when frustration gets the best of him. He uses his fists or cane. Sometimes he throws things."

Aunt Harri quit speaking. We drove in silence for a few minutes not knowing what to say. When a village traffic light stopped us, she began again: "Then the old coot calls his family and orders them to move him, complaining the staff abuse him. The kids take their parent's side, not believing the sweet old thing would hurt anyone. Gets nasty sometimes."

"What can anyone do about it?" asked Anna.

Aunt Harri just shrugged and settled back in her seat. We

reached town and took her to a fast-food outlet for a milkshake—her favourite treat. We helped her inside, selected sunny window seats, and picked up her order. Aunt Harri shed her melancholy as she sipped the shake.

"I might very well miss these milkshakes when I move on," she said brightly. "Won't miss Village Mews seniors' home. Although 'tis one of the best."

"Move?" I blurted.

"No, not move, move on. You asked me in the car what anyone could do about the problems. I know the answer for the frustrations and discomforts I face—I'll soon be moving on."

Suddenly understanding her meaning, and not knowing what to say, we changed the subject. She remained bright and talkative until we had seated her once again in the rear seat and started for Village Mews. For the next five minutes Aunt Harri said nothing, just leaned back in the seat, staring, as I thought, at the ceiling of the car.

It happened when we stopped again for the same traffic light in the village. Aunt Harri broke the silence. Without changing her position and still looking upward, she began to sing with surprising vigour in her rich mezzo voice. A passing pedestrian hearing her through the partly-open window, stopped to listen:

"Precious promise God hath given
To the weary passerby,
On the way from earth to heaven,
'I will guide thee with Mine eye'"

At that moment, the pedestrian tapped on the car window. "The light has changed. Time to move on," he said.

As we pulled away, I heard a voice from the back seat say, "Yes, soon the light will change, and I'll be moving on."

A Backward Look

On a bright, summer, Sunday afternoon, we dropped in on
Aunt Harri at Village Mews, finding her propped up on her
bed in a darkened room. Puzzled, I asked, "What are you
doing inside on such a beautiful day?"

"Heat bothers me. Light bothers my eyes. Been sitting
here remembering about cold weather in the days when I had
good eyes. When you're old you can easily creep back into
the past."

"It is hot today," I agreed. "Tell us about some of the
cool weather you remember."

"Cold, not cool. Back on the prairie farm, we had time
for fun in the winter—even when snow blocked the roads so
only horses could get through. We used to get together for
parties, for political rallies—any old excuse.

"We'd hurry through evening chores and prepare the kids
for the outing. Like our neighbours, we travelled during
winter in a horse-drawn open box mounted on runners. Fred
threw some straw on the bottom, while I got quilts and
blankets to make a cosy nest for the boys. I used to sit on a
kitchen chair near the front to keep an eye on the kids and
still watch Fred's driving. From the chair, wrapped in a travel
rug, I could just peek over the front for a view of the road
between the horses' rumps. Fred stood upright, getting a good
view but exposed to the weather.

"In the black mid-winter evening the boys would snuggle
into their nest. I'd make sure they were covered, and Fred
would holler giddyup. I'm thinking back 60 years, but I
clearly remember the sound of sleigh bells, the slapping of
harness leather, the jingling of metal fixtures, the crunch of

horses hooves on crisp snow, and the hiss of runners breaking a new track."

Aunt Harri paused for a drink of water and a moment's rest as we waited without speaking. She repositioned herself against the pillows and continued: "Often a blue-white light would dance across the sky—the northern lights. We'd stop the rig just to watch, letting the kids stand up to see clearly. It was beautiful. I am sure I could hear a whine or hum accompanying them in the stillness—heavenly music if you like. We'd move on in a few minutes, chasing the boys back under the covers. They'd soon freeze their noses at twenty degrees below zero."

"What did you do when you got to the neighbour's?" I asked.

"I'd bundle the kids into the house while Fred took the horses to the shelter of a barn or driving shed. The people would begin socializing right away. The men would play rings, throwing rubber sealer rings at a thing that looked like a dart board with cup hooks to catch the rings. The older kids would gather around a piano or try their skill on mouth organs. The women usually gathered in the kitchen and caught up on the community news. When everyone had arrived, the party or meeting would get under way, often lasting for hours."

"What did the tiny children do?" asked Anna.

"We would take them upstairs, put on their pyjamas, and place them with a row of other children across a big bed. They'd fall asleep quickly. When it came time to go, we'd wrap them up, load up the sleigh and head home. The kids would wake up next morning in their own beds."

Aunt Harri dozed off, so we tried to slip out. We got as far as the door when she called after us, "Those were great days, cold weather but warm friendly times. Thanks for listening. It's much easier to relive memories when someone listens."

A Trumpet Call

An eerie, echoing sound of a bugle woke me early in the morning. I sat bolt upright and listened. The fanfare ended in absolute stillness. Puzzled I dropped back on the pillow, but roused again as the bugle sound returned, this time with a different call, strange and far away.

"Taps," I thought. "The army call for lights out. Some idiot is practicing before most people are awake." The sound faded away as though someone had turned down a radio. I listened for a few minutes, then hearing nothing more and thoroughly awake, got up, noting the time: 6:30 a.m.

During breakfast, the phone rang. "She has gone," said a voice I didn't recognize on the other end of a noisy line.

"Who has gone?" I yelled back. "Speak up, we have a bad line."

"I'll call you back," said the voice. "Maybe we can get a better connection."

As I waited for the next call, I wondered about the identity of the 'she.' I also wondered where this 'she' might have gone, and what it had to do with me. Then I figured it out—someone had dialled a wrong number—I needn't expect another call. But before I could walk away from the phone, it rang again. This time I clearly heard a woman's voice. The woman, obviously upset, repeated, "She has gone."

"Who has gone? And who is this speaking?" I demanded.

"I am sorry. This is the superintendent from Village Mews. Harriet Brown died this morning. I thought you would want to know."

I stood silently for a moment before I could speak, "What happened? Tell me about it."

The voice at the other end had regained its composure: "She collapsed after getting up this morning. We found her on the floor in her room when she didn't come for breakfast. We put her back in bed and sent for the doctor. A few minutes later, she regained consciousness and said, 'Oh, hello.' That's all she said to us. Then she closed her eyes and began to sing. She sang one verse of a hymn, and died at 6:30 without opening her eyes again. We called the family. And I thought I should call you."

I hung up the phone. I don't believe I even thanked the superintendent for calling. Then I did exactly what I had done on three other occasions—when my mother, father, and brother died. I went for a walk, wanting to absorb the news alone.

As I walked I remembered our first meeting with Aunt Harri not five years ago. She had knocked on our door asking to borrow a hammer to assemble her bed. She stubbornly refused help then and many times later. I remembered the adventures and misadventures with the oldster. I recalled her search for a seniors' home. With tears in my eyes, I remembered witnessing her failing eyes and health.

Then with a smile on my face, I remembered her indomitable spirit. When she decided to do something, nothing stopped her. With pleasure, I reviewed her stories about the war and the years on the prairie farm. As she had got to know us, she had opened her heart to us, telling us things she had not shared with anyone else since the death of her beloved Fred nearly 40 years ago.

A feeling of satisfaction moderated my sorrow. We had befriended a lonely woman and spanned the generation gap. She had thanked us by sharing her wisdom and experience. We had gained much more than we gave, and as a result we would never be the same again.

Tears and sorrows now gone, I walked on, rejoicing in the privilege of having experienced a wonderful friendship.

ABOUT THE AUTHOR

 Ray Wiseman's early memory—being pushed up a rope ladder and over the side of a tramp steamer at age two—set the tone for his life. He has spent much time travelling, and most of his life looking from the hilltop of one adventure to the beginning of the next. Born in England, Ray has lived in British Columbia, Alberta, Saskatchewan, Ontario, and South Africa. He has travelled in Africa and Asia.

Ray counts writing as his fourth career. He began his working life as an electronics technician, then returned to school to study for the Christian ministry. He spent time in the pastorate and overseas with a missionary society. He returned to electronics, working as a video systems engineer. In 1993, he took early retirement to pursue a career as a writer and speaker and to dedicate more time to the work of Partners International.

Ray graduated from Radio College of Canada (now RCC Schools) in 1952. He has a Bachelor of Arts degree from the University of Waterloo, and a Bachelor of General and Biblical Studies from Briercrest Bible College.

Anna, his wife of over 40 years, has participated enthusiastically in his eclectic lifestyle. They have four sons and seven grandchildren.

You can contact Ray Wiseman by telephone, (519) 787-0178, or by E-mail at rsw@cyclops.empath.on.ca.

Partners International is a registered Christian non-profit organization, sponsoring school-aged children for education in the developing world, and workers and students engaged in Christian activity overseas. For additional information contact:

Partners International
8500 Torbram Rd, Unit 48
Brampton
ON L6T 5C6
Canada